Business Fundamentals
from
Harvard Business School Publishing

NEW PRODUCT DEVELOPMENT, Second Edition

HBS Publishing

CONTENTS

INTRODUCTION

Welcome to this entry in the Business Fundamentals series from Harvard Business School Publishing.

Most of the readings in this collection were developed for the MBA and executive education programs of Harvard Business School. These programs rely heavily on the case method of instruction, in which students analyze and discuss firsthand accounts of actual management situations. Students also learn the fundamentals of what managers do: how they build strategies, make choices, organize their activities, and measure performance. The fundamentals are often taught through background notes, which explain best practices, describe management tools, or analyze industries. Five such notes are the backbone of this volume on new product development. In addition, this title features a Harvard Business School case study plus three articles from journal-reprint collections that HBS Publishing distributes: *Harvard Business Review*, *California Management Review*, and *Business Horizons*.

While no Business Fundamentals title is intended as a comprehensive textbook-style presentation of the subject, we have brought breadth as well as depth to this volume, and we believe you will find that it examines trenchantly many of the essential aspects of new product development. We also strive to be current: nearly every item herein was published in the past five years.

The Business Fundamentals titles are designed for both individual study and facilitated training. If you want to use this collection of materials for self-study, we have provided a summary, outline, learning objectives, and a list of questions, ideas, and exercises for each reading to help you get started. If these readings are part of a training program in your company, you will find them to be a valuable resource for discussion and group work.

You can search for related materials on our Web site: www.hbsp.harvard.edu.

We wish you a rich learning experience!

The Editors

THE NEW PRODUCT DEVELOPMENT IMPERATIVE

(S. C. Wheelwright / #9-699-152 / 20 p)

Summary

Introduces the best practices for managing new product development projects. Includes concepts and tools related to structuring teams consistent with project objectives as well as concepts and processes for improving project execution.

Outline

Product Development Capability as a Sustaining Strategy
A Revolutionary Development Strategy--Creating the Right Set of Projects
Outstanding Project Execution--Two Imperatives
Getting on the Right Trajectory for Effective Product Development

Learning Objectives

- Understand the four basic types of product development, and the special characteristics and needs of each type
- Become acquainted with practical techniques for planning and managing product development
- Understand basic concepts and tools including project mix, project roadmap, and aggregate project plan
- Become familiar with best practices in developing and managing teams, schedules, and communications

Questions, Ideas, and Exercises

1. See Exhibit 2. How many of the "Myths" of correct product development have you been perceiving as true? Try this list out on a few trusted colleagues, but don't reveal that the myths are either correct or incorrect. How many colleagues support at least a few of these myths?

2. The new product development imperative is about the quest for growth in a competitive environment. However, one of the authors' cautionary principles might be expressed as: don't attempt too much too fast. See the section entitled "Defining the Contents of Individual Projects." In the third paragraph, note the limits on product development that most firms accept: breakthrough projects should incorporate no more than one or two major new ideas; platform projects, three to five major new features; derivative projects, a few modest modifications. Consider any new-product projects you are working on. Does your team have reasonable limits on its product-development ambitions?

3. Note the authors' coverage of teams and, in particular, Exhibit 11, "Types of Development Teams." Note especially the benefits of fitting each product-development type with the right type of team -- and the dangers of failing to do so. Based on this typology, what has your experience been with product-development teams? Were the right members chosen? Were your teams given appropriate resources and authority throughout their existence? What key lessons might your firm still need to learn about assembling and managing product-development teams?

The New Product Development Imperative

I. Product Development Capability as a Sustaining Strategy

Traditional approaches to running and growing a business favor sophisticated strategies, or perhaps marketing prowess, to bring the company to the leading edge of its industry. However, by focusing on effective new product development a compelling solution to the problem of survival and growth, with a different emphasis than the traditional one, becomes apparent. In this prescription, creating and applying the product development skills and capabilities of the firm play a central role. By continually enhancing its development capabilities, the company is able to reinvent existing product lines as well as create new ones, and thereby achieve market leadership: it beats its competitors to the market with the "right" product. The company that continually refines these capabilities creates its future. The company that doesn't may find itself reacting to competitive and market stimuli using ad hoc fire-fighting skills. Indeed, for the latter company, the time necessary to plan for the future may never be available.

The ability to systematically and quickly reinvent distinctive products and processes may be the optimal way for many companies to compete. Customer expectations, technology and competition are dynamic factors which mean that existing products will have a limited lifetime and either need to be significantly improved upon or replaced altogether. Outstanding new product development can provide a company with just the vehicle needed to meet these challenges. Through product offerings which continually evolve, a company can satisfy a dynamic rapidly changing set of customer needs and stay out in front of its competitors (see **Exhibit 1**). The smaller competitor with outstanding development capabilities (e.g. short development cycle times and effective resource allocation) can win the race against much larger, better-resourced but slower, less productive, opponents.

Research Associate Edward Smith prepared this note under the supervision of Professor Steven C. Wheelwright as the basis for class discussion rather than to illustrate either effective or ineffective handling of an administrative situation.

Exhibit 1   Forces Driving Development Imperatives

Driving Forces	Development Imperative	Implications
1. Intense competition; changing customer expectations; accelerating technological change	Fast and Responsive	Shorter development cycles; better targeted products
2. Exploding product variety; sophisticated discerning customers; technical diversity	High Development Productivity	Leverage from critical resources; increased number of successful development projects per engineer
3. Demanding customers; crowded markets; intense competition	Products with Distinction and Integrity	Creativity combined with total product quality; customers integrated with truly cross-functional development process

While the promise of product development is increasingly viewed by most managers as substantial, the reality is that development efforts most often are frustrating and disappointing both to the individuals involved as well as to senior managers. Underlying this disparity between promise and reality is a set of common misconceptions regarding the planning, direction and execution of development projects. It's not only that firms often lack a set of "*correct* principles" to guide their development work, but they systematically follow a set of "*incorrect* principles" which hamper their efforts. Examples of the latter mode of operation, and the likely outcomes, are summarized in **Exhibit 2**.

In contrast, for the company that recognizes the strategic importance of outstanding product development capabilities, and that adopts a set of efficient, effective principles to guide its development work, the benefits can be huge. To help structure management's thinking about product development, it's useful to consider the challenges as three fold. First, the company has to create the right set of development projects. Second, it has to execute those projects on target, on time and on budget. Third, the company must capture the lessons learned from each project so that capabilities for future projects are developed which enable it to respond to, or even pre-empt, changes in consumer expectations, technology, and competition. Through disciplined application of processes which support these three objectives over time, the company can become systematically better and faster at product development and play an increasingly proactive role in determining its future.

Exhibit 2   Examples of "Incorrect Principles"
                                    (Obstacles to Outstanding Development Capabilities)

Myth	A Probable Outcome if Applied
• Management should select from proposed projects.	Development strategy created by a random process – disconnected from company objectives
• Portfolio of projects should exceed capacity	Over-commitment of resources means that completed projects are late, over budget and inferior
• Dynamic environment requires frequent changes in priorities	Increasingly reactive to the environment (e.g., a competitor's moves and feigns); the company's trajectory is chaotic
• Individuals should work on multiple projects concurrently	People are over committed and ineffective; disenchantment and inefficiencies grow
• All projects should follow the same process	Putting a square peg in a round hole— projects with different needs receive the same prescription.
• Cannot compare projects— each one is unique	Experience from one project cannot be applied to another; new development projects "reinvent the wheel"
• Repeated Go/No-go reviews lead to better project results	Delays propagate through project phases; deliverables are late

II. A Revolutionary Development Strategy—Creating the Right Set of Projects

Where exactly a company chooses to pursue growth and apply its development capabilities is the starting point for defining a development strategy. Generally, there are three different areas where the company's attention can be focused: new product development, new customer development (in the existing market), or new market development. For example, when an existing product is no longer competitive, or the market in which it's sold is saturated, a company may supplant old products with new ones to maintain or increase market penetration. Alternatively, a new product designed to complement an established line can leverage existing products and broaden the company's offerings while taking advantage of existing technology, channels and customers. Or an existing product, as well as new ones, can be leveraged for entrance into a completely new market. Deciding what combination offers the best solution to the problem of sustainable profits and growth is the challenge. Increasingly, companies are finding that a set of development principles – operationalized through a series of concepts and tools – can help management address these important issues (see **Exhibit 3**).

Exhibit 3   Concepts and Tools for Creating the Development Portfolio
(8 steps towards building outstanding development capabilities)

Concepts & Tools	Description
Pre-Project	
• Characterizing project types	A common language is established by defining types of development projects; each project's contribution to the larger strategic framework becomes evident
• Strategic choice of project mix	Creating by design a development portfolio that is aligned with the company's objectives
• Creation of road maps	Linking and sequencing the individual projects in the project mix; mapping out the evolution of future product generations
• Aggregate Project Planning	The big picture: managing the strategic project portfolio
Project Execution	
• Type of project team	Building a development team that is matched to the project type; nurturing the teams that will be executing tomorrow's development projects
• Prototyping	Monitoring project performance and status relative to established targets; testing market realities and consumer acceptance
Learning from Projects	
• Project audits	Post project analysis of performance to capture know-how; creating effective processes for future development projects
• Learning across projects	Building process capabilities as a means for competitive renewal; building confidence and enabling repeated success

Tools and Concepts for a New Product Development Strategy

The first step in getting the company on the right trajectory for sustainable growth through new product development is to create a framework and terminology for thinking about and discussing development projects. This framework can help the organization recognize the patterns that emerge from past development projects and, ultimately, help the organization identify the cause-and-effect relationships which drive them. Every project is unique, yet shares common characteristics with other projects. By categorizing projects by type, the company begins building a framework which facilitates the recognition of patterns and their systematic analysis for learning.

Characterizing Project Types

Projects can vary from the small cost-cutting ones to the most radical commercialization of leading edge technology. This diversity in the degree of change can be represented by the continuum shown in **Exhibit 4**. Categorizing development projects by type can help management decide what mix of distinct development activities must be performed to launch a new product, as well as helping those working on projects to better understand their assignment and its objectives. Most firms have found that development projects can be separated into four main categories – breakthrough, platform, derivative and maintenance. Often these categories differ according to the degree of change in product technology and development know-how that each project type entails. The differences helps management understand how each of the types vary along such dimensions as scope, team size, budget, duration, etc.

Exhibit 4   Defining Development Projects
(*The development project continuum*)

BREAKTHROUGHS   PLATFORMS   MAINTENANCE

Completely new
product: Building
products and process
capabilities for the
future

Integration of new and
existing components
and processes into a
systems solution

Minor modifications:
product maintenance

Breakthrough At one end of the continuum are breakthrough projects, characterized by discrete and often disruptive changes in a product technology and the processes used to make it. A successful breakthrough project can become the basis for a seminal product line at a startup or a whole new line of products for a more mature company. For example, advances in flat panel displays and the miniaturization of computer peripheral devices in the mid 1980's enabled a manufacturer of desktop computers like Compaq, or later Dell, to bring a breakthrough product to market: the portable laptop computer. The product had significantly different technologies and manufacturing requirements from their desktop models and had to be effectively designed from scratch. The ultimate success of a breakthrough project, like the laptop, depends on a company's ability to apply new technologies and concepts and to embed them in products that customers often don't yet know they need. As a result of a breakthrough project's complexity, the duration of development activities typically extends over several years.

Platform   A platform project establishes the next generation of a product line and usually represents a systems solution to a product challenge. For example, anticipating that its laptop computer would cannibalize sales of its lowest performance desktop model, a computer manufacturer thoroughly redesigned the desktop line to make its features and performance more distinctive. The new platform would use the latest microprocessor architecture to achieve the performance boost, which in turn would require significant changes in the computer's motherboard and substantial re-engineering. Furthermore, recent technological advances in multi-media hardware and in communications protocols would be incorporated, and aesthetics would be changed to ensure product distinction from the previous desktop generation. Though technological features of the new generation platform would have much in common with the previous one (facilitating a seamless transition for customers), it represented an integration of new product functions and features, as well as the development of new manufacturing processes. As a result of the project's broad scope, a multi-functional effort would be needed to carry out the necessary development activities and would require about one and a half years to complete. Though these types of projects represent a significant investment, especially for a small company, a well-designed platform can be the foundation for derivatives for many years to come and thus should have a major impact on the company's future.

Derivative   Derivative projects are undertaken when an incremental change to an existing platform, or an existing product's manufacturing process, is required. The result may be an added feature or even reduced cost. This is a less demanding type of project since changes involved are limited in scope and require fewer resources to affect (the platform version of the product has already defined many of the development choices).   An example of a derivative project would be the introduction of a "faster" laptop computer by replacing its microprocessor with a faster version of the same chip. Another derivative based on the same platform, but "slower", could address the lower end of the market.   In this example, the derivatives are classified by the speed of the laptop's microprocessor chip (e.g. 200 megahertz versus 300 megahertz). Other simple modifications could be used to create even more derivatives however: the 350 megahertz model might come with a standard 8 gigabyte disk drive, a smaller lower cost 4 gigabyte drive, or a larger more expensive 10 gigabyte drive. The key factor is that new features can be added easily to the existing platform to specifically target the needs of smaller and smaller markets. The limited scope of derivative projects means that the development team can pursue its activities with limited supervision, relying instead on existing procedures for guidance. These types of projects can typically be completed by small functional teams in just a few months.

Maintenance   This is the simplest type of project and encompasses improvements in, or maintenance of, existing products and processes. Often this includes projects which result in increased manufacturing efficiencies, reduction of chronic low-level problems and reduction of manufacturing costs. These projects are performed by small functional teams.

While "the degree of product change" embodied in each individual development project is a primary dimension for distinguishing project types, adding one or more secondary dimensions can often provide additional insight and guidance. Possible candidates for this second dimension would include: degree of manufacturing process change, degree of delivery channel change, and degree of change required by the customer's processes. Which of these continuums will be the most helpful compliment to the primary continuum – degrees of product change – depends on the product, the market and the company's strategy.

Many manufacturing firms have found "the degree of manufacturing process change" to be a particularly useful second dimension. The result is a two-dimensional graphic as shown in **Exhibit 5**. Although an "on diagonal" project mix is not essential, it is the most prevalent. Projects in the upper right seldom are attractive, because to capture the full benefit of manufacturing process change usually requires significant product change (i.e. getting enough bang for the buck).   Projects in the lower left are infrequent, because dramatic product change generally requires significant process change in order to deliver the full power and feature benefits of the new product.

A two-dimensional display of project types can be used not only to guide the definition and discussion of future projects, but also to assess the current portfolio of projects. For example, each project might be represented by a circle and positioned on **Exhibit 5**, with the location indicating the degree of product and process change and the size of the circle indicating the amount of resources required for each project. Some companies have then found colors a useful way to show which projects are early, on time or late, or to show which projects are under, on, or over budget. Such analyses can help identify biases and trends, and focus management attention on needed improvements.

Exhibit 5 The four primary types of projects differ in the degree of change they require in product and process technology. Circles are used to indicate the location and size of individual projects within the product/process change framework.

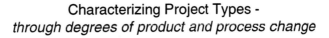

Characterizing Project Types -
through degrees of product and process change

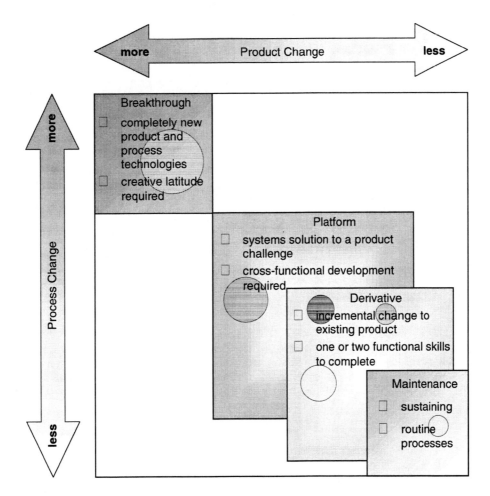

Continual Improvement of the Definitions of Project Types

For firms which have developed a process for classifying projects, many have learned over time that the definitions of project categories become even more useful as they are narrowed. Conversely, the greater the overlap between project definitions, the greater the confusion that is likely to result. When definitions are narrowed, a precise language is established that provides for efficient, effective communication with everybody "on the same page" when they plan and discuss projects.

Exhibit 6 characterizes the evolution in definitions that has occurred in many firms over time and over several generations of product.

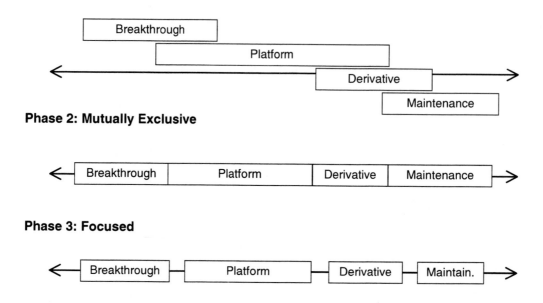

Refining Project Definitions over Time

Exhibit 6

Planning the Firm's Future as its Product Line Grows

The number of development projects and the mix of those projects that a given firm can pursue simultaneously depend on several factors. These include the resources available, the firm's strategy and even the age of the firm. For most startups, development efforts are focused initially on one major project – one that will lead to a product around which the company can build its business. Hopefully, this core product will be the basis for the firm's product line. If this core product is well designed, successful derivatives will allow the company to grow and expand the market space it can address, ultimately resulting in a stronger market position as well as a greater market share.

No matter how well designed the firm's core product is, however, it has a finite useful life span. To remain competitive, and to address a greater part of the market, the original core platform will have to be improved and possibly additional platforms with their accompanying product families will need to be added. Before long, the successful firm finds itself having to decide when (and how often) to design the next generation of an existing platform, how extensively to leverage each platform, and when (and how many) new platforms to add. These are critical development decisions because they will determine the resulting product lines offered by the company.

Paradoxically, given the need for evolving and growing product lines, most firms find themselves with far more project possibilities than their development resources will allow. Management must think carefully about the portfolio of projects that will utilize its resources effectively and provide the results called for by the firm's business strategy. One of the tools that can assist management in this effort is the creation of a project roadmap that outlines the platforms and derivatives over time and graphically illustrates their interrelationship. An example of a scenario for a desktop/laptop computer manufacturer is shown in **Exhibit 7**.

Exhibit 7　　　　This exhibit shows what the development roadmap might look like for a planned line of desktop and laptop computer derivatives based on microprocessor speed. The expected market launch and termination dates of the desktop and laptop lines are shown though the actual development projects would begin well in advance. Note that shortly after the introduction of the 350 megahertz (MHz) laptop derivative, a redesigned desktop platform would be introduced.

The Project Roadmap

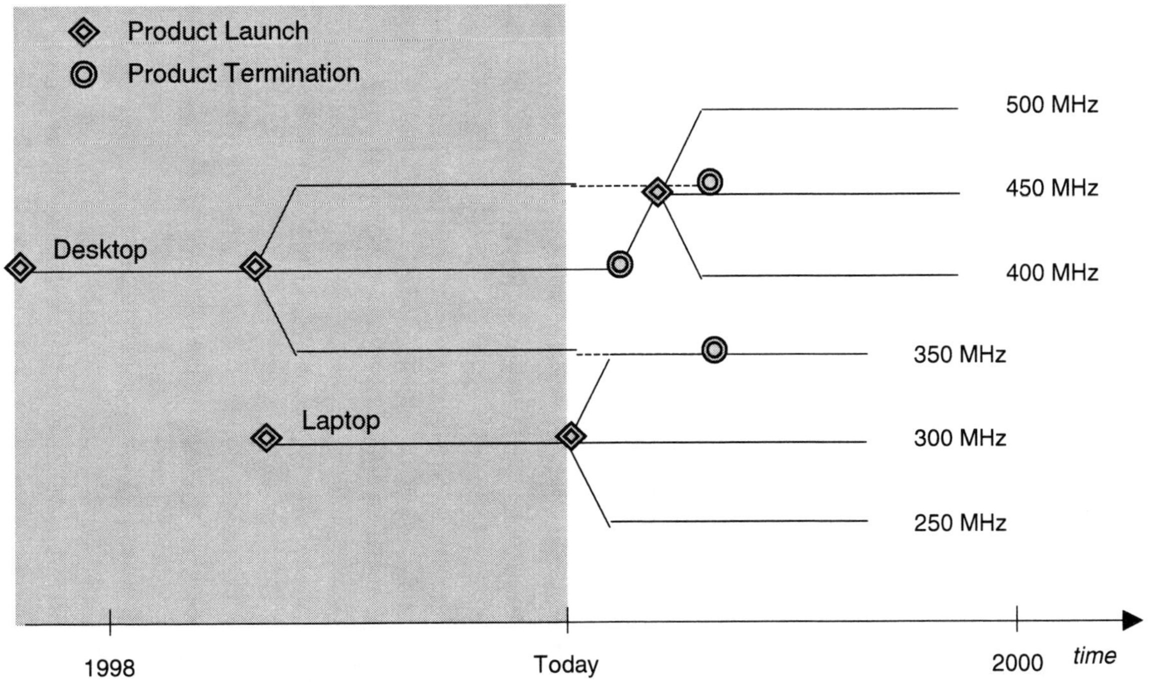

Linking Strategy to the Project Mix

The project roadmap can assist management in capturing and learning from its past development experiences, and help it in applying those lessons to future projects. Indeed, the real power of the roadmap is a prescriptive one: through a strategic choice of development projects the company can proactively determine its future sequence of projects rather than simply responding to individual project proposals. If those working on product development know the business strategy and how it translates into a project roadmap, they're much more likely to identify, define and propose projects that fit the roadmap and thus complement the strategy.

Once project types or categories are defined and narrowed within a firm, the mix of projects can be specified that will support the business strategy, and put into action the project roadmap. The project mix provides an additional tool to help management insure that the best set of projects get proposed, approved and executed. How this might work is illustrated in **Exhibit 8**. Each of the three columns – A, B, and C – represent a mix of project efforts (i.e. business strategies) tailored to a particular business. For example, in Business A, 60% of the development resources are allocated to breakthrough projects, 25% to platforms and 15% to derivatives. In contrast, Business C allocates 60% of its development resources to derivatives, 35% to platforms and 5% to breakthroughs. Business A's allocation is consistent with a high tech start-up wanting to compete on the "leading edge", whereas Company C's allocation is consistent with a strategy for a mature, broad-line business.   Company B clearly is focused on platforms with some derivatives, but limited breakthroughs.

Exhibit 8   Three different business strategies.

Achieving Business Strategy through the New Product Development Project Mix

Types of Projects	Business A Strategy	Business B Strategy	Business C Strategy
• Breakthrough	60	10	5
• Platform	25	60	35
• Derivatives & Maintenance	15	30	60
	100%	100%	100%

For each individual firm, each type of project will have a representative scope, size and duration if the firm has clearly defined each project type. Knowing those definitions, the total development budget and the desired project mix for the business, management can determine how many projects of each type it can undertake in a given period of time. For example, for a firm like Company B in **Exhibit 8**, they might find they can do 0.5 breakthroughs per year, 3.5 platforms per year, and 7.0 derivatives per year (since each derivative project is much smaller than a platform or breakthrough project). Creating the project mix, and identifying the needs by project type, will force management to address its limited resources. With a formal position established, management has a point from which an analysis of its development strategy can begin.

The Aggregate Project Plan

The purpose of the Aggregate Project Plan (APP) is to bring together the definition of project type, the overall project mix and the project roadmap. In combination, this set of tools enables management to:

- Link the set of development projects directly to the business strategy

- Fit the development efforts to the available resources

- Relate the development projects to the product lines and the markets served

- Guide decision making regarding the creation, chartering and resourcing of new projects.

Once these tools become established in a firm, management can use them to set up a schedule of anticipated new product launches. Some firms refer to this as the "development train schedule" since it establishes the timing, mix and number of "trains" (development projects) leaving the "station" (being launched by the company). **Exhibit 9** illustrates such a project schedule for CPI, a firm in the heart rhythm management business. This exhibit is specific to the CPI product lines and markets, and it accommodates the realities of the FDA approval process to which the company's products are subject. However, for CPI, it represents a major step forward in making development planning a proactive effort geared toward the firm's business strategy.

Exhibit 9
Sequencing Projects*:
Creating projects plans with rhythm and discipline

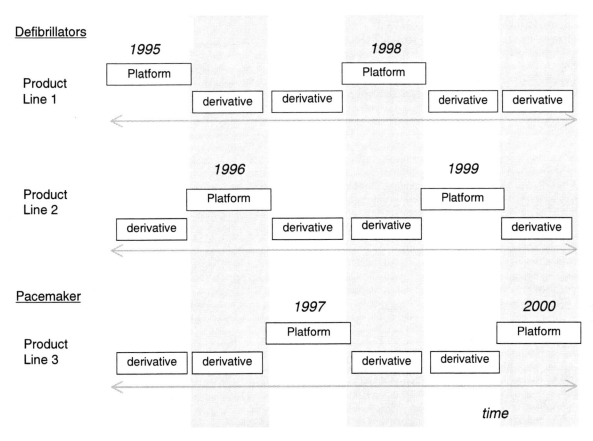

Defining the Contents of Individual Projects

Having developed a road map and aggregate project plan for the portfolio of development activities that the company desires to complete, it still remains to decide the scope and objectives of each individual project that will be pursued. This entails gathering data regarding customers, markets, competitors, and company capabilities to determine what should be the focus of each individual project. However, it also requires considerable judgment and intuition because seldom is all the information available that would be desirable.

---

* From *Cardiac Pacemakers, Inc. (A)* (see endnote)

Most firms find that a variety of approaches are needed in order to gather as much useful data as possible. Included would be customer and distributor focus groups, targeted market research studies, industry reports, advice from experts and systematic discussion among those in the firm who best know the customers. In addition, getting input from the board of directors, picking a lead customer to partner with, testing new ideas early and often with potential customers, and working with user groups can be important.

The challenge is to identify those product and system characteristics that will best meet the customer's needs and distinguish the firm's products from those offered by its competitors. However, this must be done within the bounds of a given project type as well as the firm's specific development experience. For example, most firms with a history of breakthrough products have learned that no more than one or two major new ideas should be incorporated in a single project. Furthermore, it's imperative that "proof of feasibility" be demonstrated before those new ideas are included in the project. For platform projects most firms have found that three to five major new features are the limit and that such projects most often should be thought of as next generation "systems solutions" to the customer's problems, not simply as a set of better features. Finally, derivatives need to be limited to only a few relatively modest modifications so that they can be done quickly and expeditiously in order to meet the needs of a specific large customer or a special sub-segment of the market. These principles or rules can help focus data gathering tasks in the smaller firm and reduce the likelihood of "wheel spinning" and endless "analysis/paralysis" that often occurs in larger firms.

The output of this set of activities (e.g. assembling focus groups, market research studies and vigorous dialog) should be a "charter" which guides each individual development project. While many firms choose to include selected dimensions on the desired product specifications in such charter statements, an increasing number of companies have concluded that what is most important is ensuring that the criteria for project success are clearly identified in this "determination of content phase", but that it may be undesirable to establish the specifications in too much detail. These firms have learned that detailed project specs can become too constraining in the case of breakthrough and platform projects, and may limit unnecessarily the creativity and innovativeness of the development team. For example, a platform project charter might be as specific as "success in this product will be its adoption by ten of the top twenty customers within the targeted market segment during the first twelve months following product launch, with gross margins in excess of 40%". It would then be left up to the platform development team to determine what features and content of the product would be most likely to achieve that targeted performance.

In contrast, for a derivative project the charter might be "this project will be deemed a success if it includes the highly desired feature, A, B and C, and if customers, X, Y and Z select us as their primary source of supply for this product within six months of the new product launch".

Finally, in considering the challenge of being market and customer driven in product development, it is important to recognize that the market is a moving target and the longer the project takes, the more the market will have moved. Thus building into the project execution, the need for periodic customer input and reaction to ideas and prototypes is imperative. The rule should be "get input early and often". Even when useful customer responses have been obtained and prototyping performed, however, management's judgment and intuition is also required since most customers have exhaustive wish lists, and priorities and objectives which are different from the company's. Consequently, while continual market input should be sought, it must be filtered, tested and evaluated, not simply accepted as "truth".

III. Outstanding Project Execution – Two Imperatives

Having created and approved an appropriate set of projects, project execution becomes the focus of management's attention. If pre-project activities have been done right the scope, purpose and duration of each development project will have been established. Next, the resources needed to effectively complete each project will need to be provided according to type and priority. While there are numerous tools and techniques available to assist in effective project execution, two of the most important for development projects are building a project team matched to the project type, and adopting an effective prototyping philosophy.

Creating the Right Team for the Project Type

In today's world, teams are "in". However, teams come in a variety of different forms and vary in size, expertise and often exist only as long as the individual project lasts. One way to characterize a team is by how it deals with three principle dimensions of decision making:

- The extent to which the team decides what is to be done (i.e., how tasks are carried out)

- The extent to which the team controls the resources needed to complete the project

- The nature of performance measures used to evaluate the teams and its project results

The types of teams considered for development projects can be arrayed along a continuum from functional (where those working on a project remain in their function and have only a functional role on the project) to autonomous (where the team has its own location and is its own stand-alone organizational entity). Between these two extremes are the types often referred to as "lightweight" and "heavyweight" teams. These designations reflect the extent of their authority and responsibility regarding the three dimensions highlighted above (see **Exhibit 10**).

Functional This represents a "traditional" team structure, with individual team members answerable to their respective function heads. Indeed, their placement on the team is temporary. When the project is complete, the team is disbanded. This type of team can be very effective for projects which can be subdivided into functional subprojects or on projects requiring deep technical knowledge. The team's overall performance often is not judged directly – instead each individual team member is judged by his or her functional manager based on conformance to established processes and procedures and overall "functional excellence."

Lightweight In its most common form, one functional project manager has oversight over the entire lightweight team. This adds a degree of coordination to the team's effort not often found in the functional team. However, like the functional team, individuals continue to be focused primarily on their function, not on overall project results. Individual members of a lightweight team are still answerable to their primary functions, and the project manager has little control over the resources used, the major decisions, or in establishment of targets, deadlines and performance measures.

Heavyweight Team members are still "identified" with their various functions, but their primary responsibility for the duration of the project is to the development team with each member reporting directly to the heavyweight team leader. The team leader is a "heavyweight" in the company, typically with as much authority as senior function managers. As a consequence, the team has more control over the resources used, the decisions made, and the targets established. The team is evaluated on its delivery of the project objectives.

Autonomous The autonomous team has a truly integrated cross-functional structure, and is designed to handle the most challenging development projects whose parameters are difficult to define. These teams have the most entrepreneurial spirit of the bunch — they are chartered to do what it takes to deliver the desired results. The team is given control over the resources necessary to complete the project, and usually is free to determine the team's operating procedures. It is evaluated based on results, not on adherence to processes like the functional or lightweight teams would be. The team is free to solve problems in real time and has the authority to make strategic as well as tactical decisions without bureaucracy and unnecessary overhead.

Exhibit 10 Four levels of teams are depicted here: functional, were the work is completed in the function and coordinated by functional managers (FM); lightweight, were a coordinator works through liaison representatives (L) but has little influence over the work; heavyweight, where a strong leader exerts direct, integrating influence across all functions; and autonomous, where a heavyweight team is removed from the function, dedicated to a single project, and co-located.

Types of Development Teams

1. Functional Team Structure

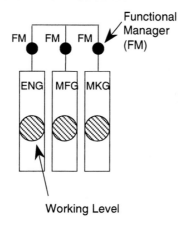

Working Level

2. Lightweight Team Structure

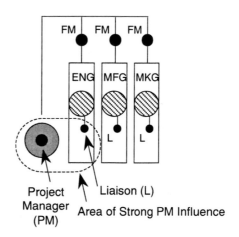

3. Heavyweight Team Structure

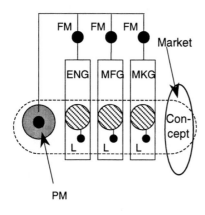

4. Autonomous Team Structure

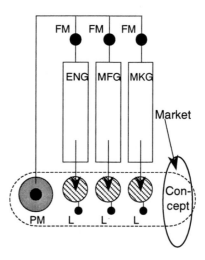

Each of these team structures has its strengths and weaknesses (see **Exhibit 11**). Based on the business strategy pursued, each company usually will have a dominant development focus with an associated dominant project type and team structure. For example, the small company betting on the commercialization of a cutting edge technology, might adapt business strategy A in **Exhibit 8**, and choose to have 60% of its resources committed to a breakthrough project: with the dominant team structure being autonomous. In such circumstances, the development team is likely to be a primary driver of much of the company's activities. Thus the team has great latitude and influence on decision making, with other parts of the company organized to support its efforts.

Exhibit 11

Project Team Types
(*Their strengths and weaknesses*)

Team Structure and Associated Characteristics	Strengths	Weaknesses
Functional (traditional): Team members work under different functional managers; projects evolve in a serial fashion as tasks pass from one function to the next.	• Brings functional expertise to problem solving • Function managers control resources for the tasks they own	• Judged based on adherence to function processes rather than overall project results • Lack of coherence between functional tasks on complex projects; serial processing • Cookie cutter approach to solving varied problems
Lightweight: Heightened degree of coordination due to "administrative" oversight; similar to a functional team	• Same as functional • Oversight of collective functional responsibilities helps ensure timely project completion	• Same as functional • The lightweight manager has little organizational clout and little power to affect critical decisions
Heavyweight: Core team members are representatives of their functions on an integrated development team; heavyweight manager is a heavyweight in the organization	• Heavyweight manager has broad control over the decision-making processes, resources used and targets established	• Team members still report to functional head; rewards and responsibilities are disconnected from project deliverables • Political tightrope - project manager has about the same stature as functional heads
Autonomous: Team members are co-located and answer only to the heavyweight project manager; the team has extreme latitude to devise solutions to the problems it has responsibility for.	• Focus: no conflicting forces pulling at team members • Speed and ability in solving challenging, novel problems • Complete functional integration- the broadly skilled team is independent	• Less corporate control; team tends to expand on original project description • Little use of existing process solutions • Unique product and process solutions may be difficult to integrate into existing business

Conversely, a larger company with more than one established product line might following business strategy B. Their focus is on a series of platform projects with each being staffed with a strong heavyweight team. Strong project management, as well as collaboration with the functions, ensures that the new platform being developed will be aligned with the company strategy, yet make effective use of existing processes and technologies. The heavyweight, as well as the autonomous, teams have market responsibilities within their scope of accountability (see **Exhibit 10**), which is essential if they are to be judged on market results.

Finally, a firm pursuing business strategy C (typically a large firm with multiple existing platform-based product lines) would likely do many derivative projects with only an occasional breakthrough or platform effort. Their primary organization structure is likely to be functional, making it natural for them to use mainly functional and lightweight development teams. Such a company would have the option of using an autonomous team when pressed to do a breakthrough or platform project.

Effective Communication: Schedules and Timing

Once a project is underway, both the team and senior management need a way to track and respond to project progress. While a defined process that breaks the development effort into phases and milestones is very useful, equally important for breakthrough and platform projects is providing timely information on the status of key aspects of the project. Chris Meyer has proposed the concept of a dashboard as one way to do this (see **Exhibit 12**). This comprehensive indicator, much like the dashboard in a car or plane, displays for both project members and company management alike the status of key activities in the project. Many companies have found this a particularly useful tool for development project management.

Exhibit 12　　　　　The Project Team Dashboard*
(A comprehensive performance indicator at one company)

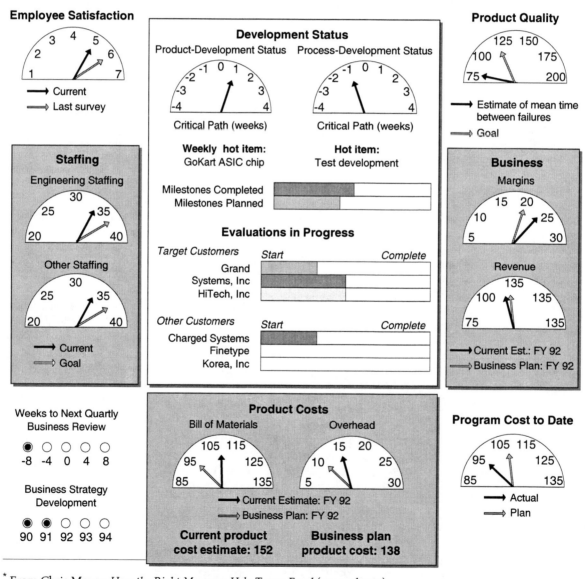

* From Chris Meyer, *How the Right Measures Help Teams Excel* (see endnote)

Linking Development Project Phases to Prototype Cycles

One other tool that has exceptional leverage in executing development projects, but which is often underutilized, is prototyping. A prototype cycle consists of three steps – design, build and test (DBT). Early in a project, prototypes may be simple mockups, simulations or breadboards, whereas later on they may involve pilot production builds.

The DBT cycle embedded in prototyping is a critical tool for helping determine what design will best meet customer needs and how the company can best produce and deliver that product. It does this by providing a representative model for testing not only the product's physical and functional attributes, but enables customers to provide specific feedback, facilitating the company's own development of its operating processes and procedures. It also is a communications tool, between various functions and between the development team and management. When prototyping occurs in conjunction with each phase of the project, it provides an excellent reality check on the status of the project, what is and isn't resolved, and how well the project is progressing towards targeted objectives.

For most firms, prototyping is a grossly underutilized tool for managing development projects. By better planning and execution of more frequent prototype cycles, a team can quicken the pace at which it moves to a final design, and increase the likelihood of success by using it as a vehicle to gather ongoing customer input (by letting them review and evaluate prototype units) and to test the rest of the organization's readiness to support and deliver this new product.

Project Staffing and Career Development

Human resources selection, training, and development policies need to complement the future development strategy of the company (e.g. provide the right mix and quality of skills for the company to meet its development objectives). For many companies, when it comes time to staff a development project they find they have a major shortage of people with the breadth and experience called for.

Development projects can be used not only to create new products, but to train people and build the breadth and depth of their skills in important managerial and functional areas. Less experienced employees, or newly hired ones, often start on derivative projects where job functions tend to be narrower and less complex. Next, they might move onto platform projects as a core team member where they represent both their function and the team. Then they might be assigned to lead a development team on a derivative project. Finally, they might be asked to lead a major project. On-the-job training and associated career development paths are an essential tool for a company wishing to create a significant capability in new product development.

Critical in staffing development projects is having a qualified cadre of project leaders. This is especially critical for the execution of platform projects where several functions and a comprehensive set of tasks must be integrated and managed. In recent years, many firms have adopted heavyweight team structures for such projects. However, far too often they've failed to select a heavyweight project leader with the requisite experience, skills and credibility. Shown in **Exhibit 13** are several of the characteristics that distinguish heavyweight project managers, and when present, do much to assure the success of a project.

Exhibit 13   Project managers take on a variety of roles and responsibilities, eleven of which are depicted here. How much of a heavyweight (versus lightweight) project manager's role occurs on a specific project is determined by how extensive a role the project manager takes in each of these areas.

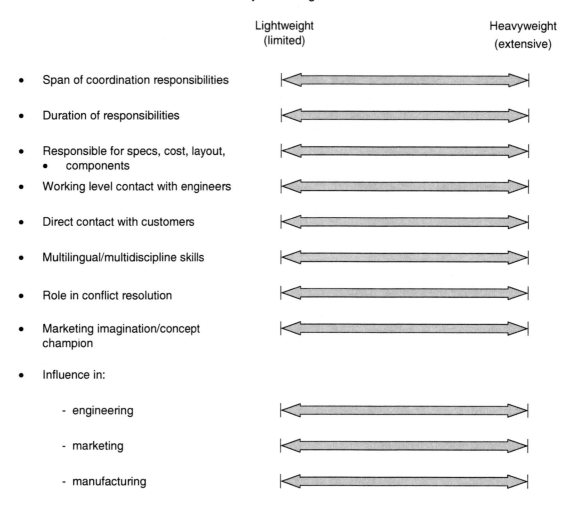

Project Manager Profile

IV. **Getting on the Right Trajectory for Effective Product Development**

Having put into effect a pre-project planning process that "creates" the right set of projects, and having established a set of procedures that consistently executes individual projects on time, on budget and on target for the market, it remains for senior management to establish a virtuous learning cycle. That is, management must identify ways to capture the learning from individual development projects – through post-project audits, systematic training, new tools and procedures, etc. – and apply it to new projects.

Recent studies contrasting more effective development with less effective development indicates that firms in the former category not only turn out more new products in a given time period, but they put themselves on a much steeper improvement trajectory, as shown graphically in

Exhibit 14. While customers buy the products and services created by these firms, what makes their advantage sustainable is the fact that every project significantly improves the development capabilities of the firms.

Exhibit 14   This example compares two competitors who incorporate similar amounts of technological change in each generation of product, but the slow competitor lets twice as much time elapse between product generation introductions as does the faster one.   Note the fast cycle competitor starts one year after the slow cycle competitor .

Getting on the Right Development Trajectory

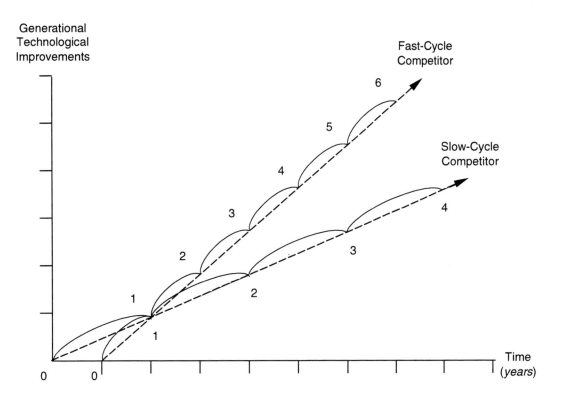

References and Additional Readings

New product and process development

1. For a detailed and comprehensive resource on new product and process development: Kim B. Clark, Steven C. Wheelwright, *Managing New Product and Process Development: Text and Cases*, The Free Press, 1993

2. For an overview on the importance of new product development capabilities and planning future projects: H. Kent Bowen, Kim B. Clark, Charles A. Holloway, Steven C. Wheelwright, *Development Projects: The Engine of Renewal*, Harvard Business Review, **94501**, September-October 1994

3. *Process-Based Capabilities: A Principal Focus of Operations Management*, Harvard Business School Publishing, 1995

Project planning

4. Two references for effective new product and process design in development projects: Karl T. Ulrich, *Product Design and Development*, McGraw-Hill Inc., 1995; Dan L. Shunk, *Integrated Process Design and Development*, Business One Irwin, 1992

5. Steven C. Wheelwright, W. Earl Sasser, Jr., *The New Product Development Map*, Harvard Business Review **89315** May-June 1996

6. Steven C. Wheelwright, Kim Clark, *Creating Project Plans to Focus Product Development,*, Harvard Business Review, **92210**, March-April 1992

7. Ellen Stein, Marco Iansiti, Thomas J. Kosnick, *Product Development: A Customer Driven Approach*, Harvard Business School Publishing, **695-016**, 1996

8. The following source provides the latest thinking in the area of customer focus in product development: Edward F. McQuarrie, *Customer Visits: Building a Better Market Focus*, Sage Publications, 2nd ed., 1998

Project execution and management

9. Kim B. Clark, Steven C. Wheelwright, *Organizing and Leading Heavyweight Development Teams*, California Management Review, Spring 1992

10 For a detailed look at concepts and tools for project management: *Project Management Manual*, Harvard Business School Publishing, **697-034**, 1996

11. Christopher Meyer, *How the Right Measures Help Teams Excel*, Harvard Business Review, **94305**, May-June 1994; For an effective use of the dashboard concept during a development project, see *Chrysler and BMW: Tritec Engine Joint Venture*, Harvard Business School Publishing, **699-033**, 1998

12. Steven C. Wheelwright, Mikelle F. Eastley, *Cardiac Pacemakers, Inc. (A)*, Harvard Business School Publishing, **698-024** 1998

13. *Constructing and Using Process Control Charts*, Harvard Business School Publishing, **686-118**, 1986

14. For a more detailed view on the operation manager's role in process development and project coordination, please look at: Ananth Raman, *Coordination: An Overview*, Harvard Business School Publishing, **696-001**, 1995; Ann E. Gray, *Process Fundamentals*, Harvard Business School Publishing, **696-023**, 1997

Learning from development project execution and management

15. Joseph L. Bower, Thomas M. Hout, *Fast-Cycle Capability for Competitive Power*, Harvard Business School Publishing, **88602**, November-December 1988

PRODUCT DEVELOPMENT:
A CUSTOMER-DRIVEN APPROACH

(M. Iansiti and T.J. Kosnik / #9-695-016 / 22 p)

Summary

This note introduces managers to the basics of product development: concept development, product design, and methodologies for investigating user needs.

Outline

Laying the Foundation
  The Product Development Funnel
  A Complementary View: The Stage-Gate Model
  Assessing Market Potential
  Selecting and Managing the Development Team
Developing the Product
  Preparing for Concept Generation
  Concept Generation
  Concept Selection
  Product Engineering and Design
  Prototyping
  Pilot Production and Ramp Up and Market Launch

Learning Objectives

- Build knowledge necessary to evaluate the effectiveness of a new product development process
- Become familiar with common methods for understanding user needs and screening product concepts
- Identify stakeholders for a new product and understand the relationships among them

Questions, Ideas, and Exercises

1. Review the two approaches to product development shown in Figures 1 and 2. Then sketch out the product-development process used in your unit. In two or three sentences, describe your process and its underlying logic. How does it compare with the product-development funnel and the stage-gate model? What stages in your product-development process receive disproportionate time and resources? What steps or stages do not receive adequate attention? Describe the actions you and your colleagues could take to strengthen this process.

2. Consider a market forecast for a new product. Outline a plan for how you will respond if actual demand is either much greater or much slighter than forecast. Be sure your plan addresses relationships with key constituencies, including:

- Manufacturing
- Sales and marketing
- Suppliers
- Distributors

Identify a colleague in each constituency with whom you will share this plan and ask for feedback.

3. "We refer to all groups with a stake in the development, existence, and obsolescence of a product as 'stakeholders'," say the authors.

(a) List as many stakeholders as you can think of for a new product you are working on. Remember to list not just the obvious stakeholders but also anyone who is likely to use or come into contact with the product at every stage of its life cycle.

(b) Prioritize your list of stakeholders. Decide which ones have the greatest stake in the "development, existence, and obsolescence" of the product and briefly note the reasons why.

(c) Identify which stakeholders' needs are likely to conflict with those of others. How will you ensure that your knowledge of potentially conflicting needs will be communicated in the next stages of concept generation?

Product Development:
A Customer-Driven Approach

Introduction

No well-intentioned company would try to develop a product that did not succeed in the marketplace, but stories of product failures in fact abound. Sometimes the product or service may be sound but marketing and distribution issues destroy its chances for success. In other cases, the product or service itself may not meet users' latent and stated requirements. What can be done during the development process to assure that the output successfully exhibits the qualities that customers want to see? Put in simple terms, if a company uncovers what customers want, designs a product that meets those needs, and is able to build and distribute it at an acceptable cost, the company will succeed – although there are innumerable ways in which that simple formula can fail. This note will address the issues of product development broadly and suggest how to improve the probability of a project's success.

Laying the Foundation

The Product Development Funnel

A helpful way of thinking about product development is to view the process as a funnel (see **Figure 1**). The widest opening, indicating the point of maximum flexibility, exists at the beginning of the project. As the project evolves, the company commits to specific concepts, product designs, and manufacturing processes. This reduces the options available to the product developers, i.e., the funnel narrows.

Before "entering" the project funnel, company management needs to address questions of the project's scope (e.g., basic project objectives, profitability, introduction date) and the resources it will likely consume. More often than not, companies have more projects underway than they can possibly complete with the available resources in the desired time frame. As a result, no project should be approved until the entire portfolio of projects has been considered and the real feasibility of completing all these efforts has been assessed. And when companies face rapidly changing market conditions, projects initially approved to enter the product development funnel

Research Associate Ellen Stein prepared this note under the supervision of Professor Marco Iansiti and Visiting Professor Thomas J. Kosnik as the basis for class discussion rather than to illustrate either effective or ineffective handling of an administrative situation.

may subsequently have to be abandoned, based on market intelligence gained later in the development process.

Figure 1: The Product Development Funnel

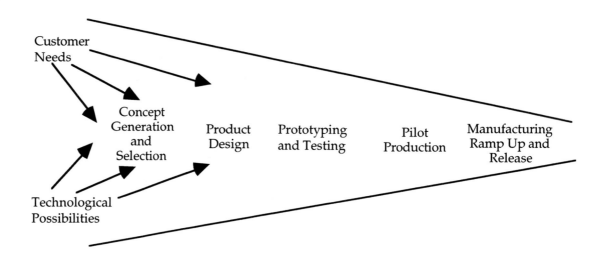

A Complementary View: The Stage-Gate Model

Another view of the new product development process used in some organizations is a Stage-Gate Model. This conceptualization of the process identifies a series of development stages, similar to those shown in the product development funnel. It complements the product development funnel by explicitly identifying a series of gates through which a new product project must successfully pass on its journey from initial idea to full commercial launch.

Each gate is a go/no-go decision. At each gate, the new product project can be compared with other projects in the company's new product funnel that are competing for scarce development resources. A company often must decide to put some projects on the "back burner," or even to cancel projects, based on information about changing customer needs, technology, or competitive activity.

A Stage-Gate Model creates discipline in the process by requiring a periodic systematic review of every project in the pipeline at multiple milestones in its development cycle. This allows management of a company to "pull the plug" on new product projects that may have seemed like a good idea at the beginning, but that are less attractive as new information becomes available. By periodically "thinning the herd," a company increases the chances for success of projects that remain in the funnel, by ensuring that they will receive the resources they need to move rapidly through the development process to market launch.

Figure 2 is a schematic of a Stage-Gate Model that has been developed by Cooper.[1] It is important to note that although the Stage-Gate Model appears to be a linear sequence of activities, most companies with effective product development processes allow for cross functional teams to work on parallel, overlapping tasks throughout a project. For example, a project team may develop tentative plans for testing and validation (stage 4) and full production (stage 5) before a project has

---

[1] See Cooper, "Stage-Gate Systems: A New Tool For Managing New Products".

passed through Gate 3 or Gate 4. However, if a product fails at one of those gates, the plans for later stages are not implemented.

Figure 2: The Stage-Gate Model of New Product Development

Initial Screen	Second Screen	Decision on Business Case	Post-Development Review	Pre-Launch Business Analysis	Post-Implementation Review

Idea → G1 → S1 → G2 → S2 → G3 → S3 → G4 → S4 → G5 → S5 → PIR

Ideation	Preliminary Investigation	Detailed Investigation (build business case)	Development	Testing & Validation	Full Production & Market Launch

Why are the product development funnel and the Stage-Gate Model important? First, because they offer complementary tools to help guide new team members through the seemingly chaotic process of their first new product development process. Second, because they allow management of a company to manage the many projects in their new product portfolio in a dynamically changing environment, and to make decisions that optimize the allocation of resources across projects as markets evolve. Third, because they create expectations among those that work in the new product development process that not every good idea will necessarily reach the market. This may reduce the disappointment among project team members who invest their time and energy in a project, only to have it postponed or canceled. Finally, these tools can be used to diagnose potential problems in the product development process. For example, a product development funnel with too wide a mouth might symbolize a process where too many ideas are allowed to start the process. A Stage-Gate Model with a gate that only 1% of the projects survive might indicate a screening process that is so risk-averse that it is excessively constrains a company's capacity for innovation.

Assessing Market Potential

At the outset of a new product development project, a preliminary assessment must be made of the potential demand for the new product or service. The estimate of market potential is revised and refined with the most current information about costs, competition, technology, and market needs at every gate of the Stage-Gate Model. The assessment of market potential is closely linked to the selection of the market segment that a new product will serve. Why is the choice of target market so important? A CEO of a leading microcomputer software company (who wishes to remain anonymous) put it best:

> It usually takes about the same amount of development time and talent to design a product that will meet the needs of one hundred customers as a product that will meet the needs of one million. Since talented product developers are usually a scarce resource, most shareholders, customers, and employees would prefer that a company leverage that resource to meet the greatest need. For any business that aspires to grow and prosper, picking the right market segment is the most critical decision in the product development process.

There are numerous sophisticated tools and techniques for estimating size and growth potential of a product category, or the market share of a new entrant that aspires to challenge existing competitors. For example, SAMI/Burke, a marketing research firm, offers a family of computer models called BASES that forecast the market potential of new consumer product concepts based on surveys with consumers before a product has been physically produced. BASES has been used by an impressive list of marketing companies, including Colgate Palmolive, Frito-Lay, Gillette, Nestlé, and Procter & Gamble.[2] In one case, Nestlé Refrigerated Foods Company used the BASES II test, which involved a concept test in combination with a product taste test, to develop a rigorous forecast of market demand during the development of their highly successful Contadina brand refrigerated pastas and sauces.[3]

For start-up companies without the resources to afford extensive market research, or situations where a product may be the first of its kind, such as Sony in portable tape players and Xerox in copiers, there are simpler techniques for estimating demand. Most make creative use of secondary data that is relatively inexpensive to acquire, and is often free via libraries, government agencies, and so forth. A few basic approaches for estimating market demand are shown below:

- Population-based estimates: These estimates involve taking the total population, number of households, number of companies, and so forth, and estimating the percentage that will buy in a product category each year. This technique is often used for consumer durables such as color televisions, cellular phones, or automobiles. For a new product category, there are numerous models that predict the number of units bought over time will resemble an S-shaped curve, whose slope depends on the percentage of the population that are "innovators" and "imitators" (who buy partially because they saw that someone else had purchased), and the saturation point (the total percentage of the population that will buy over the product category's life cycle).

- Population * usage-based estimates: For product categories that have a short interval between purchases, such as cola drinks, coffee, and toilet paper, the market size in any year is a function of the number of customers (individuals or households) multiplied by the number of purchase occasions per year, and the average number of units purchased on each occasion.

- Forecasting by analogy: For new product categories without an existing track record, examining the market size of similar products in the first few years of their life cycle offers a baseline for the new product. For example, a company estimating the market for a new movies-on-demand service via the information superhighway might examine the early growth records of cable movie channel subscriptions, such as Showtime, Cinemax, and Home Box Office, to determine how many households might become customers of movies-on-demand each year for the first several years.

- Forecasting by percentage of complementary product sales: For example, the creators of a new software program for notebook computers might assume that they could achieve a percent penetration of all new notebook computers sold, and take advantage of secondary research data on the number of notebook computers that will be sold in the next few years. Similarly, the number of bicycle helmets might be tied to bicycle sales.

- Forecasting based on past competitor performance: In product categories where other companies have established a track record, estimating a new entrant's share of the market can be based partially on the experience of competitors. For example, if only one in ten new products in a category has

---

[2] See Dolan, *Managing the New Product Development Process,* for more detail

[3] For more details about Nestlé's use of BASES II, see "Nestlé Refrigerated Foods (A): Contadina Pasta & Pizza," Harvard Business School Case 9-595-035.

been successful, and if there are data available about the investment that various competitors have made in trying to launch new products, as well as first year unit sales for different launches, a company can build a pragmatic estimate of the range of sales that a new product might enjoy in best case, expected, and worst case scenarios.

The five approaches above suggest that a quick-and dirty estimate of market potential for a new product category and for a new brand in an existing category can be done with a minimal investment of time and money. The irony is that a task that is relatively straightforward is often wildly inaccurate. Many prognostications have erred on the side of over-optimism; consider, for example, the forecasts of demand for eight track tape systems in the 1960s, or artificial intelligence software in the 1980s. However, there are also a fair number of overly-pessimistic forecasts that have resulted in an inability to manufacture sufficient quantities and a loss of market share to competition. IBM's tendency to underestimate demand for its microcomputers, leading to product shortages, has been one reason for Compaq's success from the 1980s through the present day.

What lessons can we learn from all of this? First, estimating market potential is essential. Second, we should be willing to challenge our own forecasts, or those of our suppliers and customers. Third, we should plan for contingencies so that if the demand for our new product is ten times less or ten times more that we had anticipated, we have a game plan to respond to the voice of the marketplace as it makes itself heard during the new product launch. Finally, we should reduce cycle time in new product development, manufacturing, and delivery so that we can develop and deliver products we know customers will buy – because they've already ordered them in advance.

Selecting and Managing the Development Team

Once the development process is understood, the formation and operation of the development team are critical to the project's outcome. Numerous factors influence optimal team composition, including company size, reporting structure, geographical proximity of employees, product nature (e.g., technical, marketing-driven), available resources, and so forth. In most environments small, cross-functional teams are recommended if possible.[4] In addition, it is important to create incentives for the team members to work collaboratively, and infrastructure to help the team communicate and work effectively across barriers of time, distance, and cultural differences that might otherwise inhibit its effectiveness.

Developing the Product

Once the development team has been selected and the project scope defined, actual product development can begin. By this point, general issues of target markets and financials have been addressed in the project scope definition, but no specifics about the product itself should have been outlined. That discussion is initiated through the concept-generation process.

Preparing for Concept Generation

A product concept addresses the question of how the product will meet stakeholder needs by describing, usually through a drawing or rough three-dimensional model and some general text, what technology and form the product will employ. Before that sketch or description can be created, however, the needs that the product will fulfill have to be uncovered. For this to happen, a decision must be made about whose needs will be met.

---

[4] See Wheelwright and Clark, *Revolutionizing Product Development*, Chapter 8.

Who Are the Stakeholders?

Quite often, companies think of getting input only from "the customers," i.e., from those who either make the buying decision and/or actually use the product. Yet in almost all product development projects, rarely is only one voice to be heard; more than one group of people has to be considered, although not every group needs to be considered to the same degree. We refer to all groups with a stake in the development, existence, and obsolescence of a product as "stakeholders." For example, stakeholders in the development of a bedside heart monitor used in hospitals would include the various groups within the company producing the product (e.g., manufacturing, design, shipping, purchasing), the administrators within the hospital who are concerned with how much the goods cost, doctors and nurses who deploy the device, patients who will be hooked up to it, and service people who will have to fix it if there is a problem. And even this is not a complete list. Hospital maintenance people who must dispose of the cardboard boxes in which the units are shipped have a stake in the existence of the product, as do the people who decide what should be done with the monitors once they are replaced by newer technology. Again, the voices of all stakeholders should be not be given equal weight, but in the event that their needs conflict, compromises can be deliberately made – and in some cases may be avoided entirely.

What Information Should You Gather from the Stakeholders?

Figuring out what to ask stakeholders once these people have been determined depends primarily on the undertaking. Is it an entirely new business for the corporation, requiring a hefty amount of resources, or is it a slight modification to something already being produced? In the first situation, if the company is unfamiliar with many of the issues surrounding the product (e.g., how the customer behaves, how purchasing decisions are made, how distribution channels operate) it will want to do some broad, qualitative searching before it delves into product-specific issues in its inquiries. The more empathetic the team members are toward the product's stakeholders, the higher the likelihood that the company will introduce a satisfying product, since essentially it will be able to critique the product just as eventual customers would. Such ability to understand what pleases and displeases stakeholders will be particularly useful during the design process, for almost certainly design tradeoffs will needed. If the team *truly* understands the context and manner in which the product is to be distributed, sold, used, and disposed of, it will be able to make better decisions and knowledgeable choices among options.

Once this empathic portion of the investigation has been conducted, the team can ask more pointed questions about the particulars of the product to be developed. In all parts of the investigation, the team should keep in mind *when* the product is going to be introduced – i.e., the lag time between assessing stakeholder needs and actual product introduction. There may be important issues at product introduction that are not understood or uncovered at the time of the inquiry. These must be addressed at some point during the overall exploration of customer needs.

Sometimes a product is new not only to the company but to the marketplace. When Sony introduced the Walkman, for example, no comparable offering was available to the general population. When this is the case, those interviewing stakeholders may have to explain their questions carefully or frame them in various ways, since respondents may not be able to visualize or verbalize what they want. For example, if a team wants to develop an entirely new recreational, mechanical transportation device that is not a bicycle, it may have to ask questions about lifestyle, environment, storage space, and mechanical dexterity without ever addressing product-related features, since many respondents might not be able to imagine anything other than a bicycle.

The most effective interactions with stakeholders are through direct observation and personal interviews and ideally should be conducted in the setting in which the product will be used. Quite often it is difficult to gain a real sense of what respondents want or need unless the context in which they will be using the product is appreciated. A cardiac nurse might talk about features of heart monitor alarms that should go off when a patient exhibits arrhythmia. Unless the product developer understands the noisiness of the hospital unit in which the monitor may be used, however, she may not make the right decisions about what the alarms should sound like and how loud they should be. Of course, if the product is considered an enhancement or if the application is fairly well understood, less effort is necessary in conducting extensive qualitative investigations or doing so in the actual setting of use. In general, determining what particular form of interaction to employ will depend on the nature of the questions, the accessibility of the desired respondents, and the time and resources available to the team.

What Do You Do with the Information You Gathered?

Ideally, the data-gathering stage should produce unedited statements from the respondents, general impressions from the interviewers, and quantitative results from surveys, without interpretation or bias. An excerpt of what a team developing a sleeping bag might have to work could include the following:

> I've had my sleeping bag for 24 years and it hasn't let me down yet. I keep it in my car for those times I'm on the road and just feel like goin' and goin'. Where I end up, I sleep! (40 year old male, hiked the Appalachian Trail 2 times, works as a cook in a restaurant to support his climbing and hiking activities.)

> I know I'm supposed to take good care of my sleeping bag, but that doesn't make me do it. The thing stays stuffed in its little bag when its not in use. (20 year old college female; uses bag indoors when there aren't enough beds, and about 1 week per summer camping in the West.)

> The users we're looking at are simple, unpretentious, and not too much into image when it comes to sleeping bags. The label on the product only means something if it indicates reliability and quality. They're much more concerned with performance (weight, warmth). (Thoughts of the interviewer.)

Working together, the team should go through the list responses, removing statements that do not make sense, clarifying those that have more than one possible interpretation, separating remarks with more than one message into different points, and eliminating duplicate sentiments. Once this has been done, those touching on the same ideas can be grouped and assigned a single summarizing statement. This summarizing should be done repeatedly until the highest or most abstract level is a more manageable group of about 30 user needs that can be consulted throughout the rest of the process. The original statements should not be discarded, however; if a question about what the user groups really wanted subsequently arises, the information can be reviewed for clarification.

In an ideal world, a product would meet the needs of all stakeholders at an acceptable price. In reality, however, technological, logistical, and financial constraints usually demand that some tradeoffs and compromises be made in the design process. Thus to decide which needs are critical and which are less important, their relative and absolute weights have to be determined.

The *relative* weight can be assigned by having users rank order a list of the summary needs. The *absolute* value of each need can be assessed through a technique called the Kano[5] method. By asking and analyzing questions about the user needs in a particular way (see **Appendix A** for more details), each need can be assigned a label – must have, linear satisfier, delighter, and indifferent, which are defined as follows:

> *Must Have* – no matter how well the product meets the need, the customer simply accepts it as something expected. However, if the need is not met, the customer is very dissatisfied.

> *Linear Satisfier* – the better the product is at meeting the need, the better the customer likes it.

> *Delighter* – if the product fails to include this, the customer is not unhappy. But while its absence does not cause dissatisfaction, its presence will increase customer satisfaction.

> *Indifferent* – the need produces neither satisfaction nor dissatisfaction in the consumer, regardless of whether or not it is met in the product.

Once a label has been assigned to each need, subsequent design tradeoff decisions can be made more intelligently. For example, the development team designing a new all-season tent for serious hikers will encounter a conflict between weight and durability. A sturdier tent able to withstand all types of wind, snow, and rain conditions will come at the cost of higher weight (not to mention more expensive material costs). In deciding how much durability to build into the product, the team would be helped by knowing that the user need "the tent will withstand any weather that I may encounter" is considered a "must have" by 80% of respondents, while "the tent must not be too heavy" is a "must have" in the eyes of about 40%. Obviously, "too heavy" has to be clarified, but the point is that the "must have" condition should be met given its importance to such a high percentage of respondents.

Concept Generation

Translating Customer Needs into Product Features

Once the information has been prioritized, one more step is necessary: translating the customer's vocabulary into a form that engineers and others can use. For example, what does it mean to a designer when a customer says, "I want to be able to totally stuff my backpack and throw it around without having it open up on me?" How will the designer know that she has satisfied this need? Some sort of metric must be set up with a corresponding target value so the development team can continually evaluate whether the product it is developing is meeting the user needs. (Note: when choosing the target values, it is useful to benchmark existing products – those within the company and from competitors – to determine what the new product should provide.) Most likely, preliminary specifications will have to be modified as prototypes are built and the feasibility and desirability of the chosen values are evaluated.

In the backpack example, the metric might be that the pack should be able to withstand a certain amount of force while stuffed to the very limits of its capacity. It is important at this point that *solutions* to the needs *not* be incorporated into the product specifications. For instance, those who have previously used packs with zippers might translate the above customer need into a specification that the zippers be of a certain strength. But zippers are only one way of closing the bag and therefore should not yet be assumed to be part of the design.

Translating customer needs into product attributes by assigning metrics is helpful when employing a technique called Quality Function Deployment (QFD). QFD uses various "houses"

---

[5] Named for its creator, Professor Noriaki Kano.

that have information arranged in matrix form, visually representing correlations among particular attributes (which in turn depend on the specific house). The first house, called the House of Quality, contains the information discussed above (i.e., the customer needs as rows and the product attributes or specifications as column headers). **Figure 2** provides a simplified version of the House of Quality for the development of a travel mug.

Figure 2: Simplified House of Quality – Travel Beverage Mug

User Needs	Size and Shape of Mouth Opening	Shape of Handle	Insulating Material	Outside Material	Capacity
Shouldn't cause dribble down front of shirt	++	+		+	
Should keep liquid hot for at least one hour	-		++	+	-
Should have comfortable feel	+	++		+	
Should be low cost			–	–	-
Should not spill if knocked on its side	–				

Product Specifications

++ = strong positive correlation
+ = positive correlation
- = negative correlation
-- = strong negative correlation

What Is a Concept?

Until this point, the team's focus should be strictly upon the questions of "who" and "what": Who are the critical stakeholders? What do the stakeholders want? What should the product offer to meet those demands? The question of "how" should have been avoided so that the design options would not be prematurely limited. Once the "what" questions have been answered, however, solutions can be evaluated, primarily through the creation of product concepts.

The distinctive combination of the answers for the "who," "what," and "how" questions is a product concept's positioning statement, where:

Positioning = Differentiation (what + how) + Segmentation (for whom).

In addition to the verbal positioning statement, a product concept should illustrate, through the use of text, drawings, and models, the product's performance and technical features; how it should be configured or architected, how it should serve customers, who those customers are, and its meaning to those customers (e.g., status, personality, feel, image).[6] Product concepts may be described in objective measures, such as speed, size, horsepower, and the like; in emotional,

---

[6] See Clark and Fujimoto, *Product Development Performance.*

subjective terms suggesting how the product should make customers feel; or as a combination of emotional and measurable criteria. The purpose of the product concept is to give the entire development team a common set of objectives upon which to act. Since members of even the most interactive team will make a fair number of decisions on their own, they all must have the same goals in mind if their individual choices are to support each other.

One illustration of a product concept is that created by a group of Harvard Business School students for a class project. The students were working with a large electronics company to develop a product that would be introduced to the "home communicator market" within a two-year time frame. Their extremely vague charter was to create a product to address all the communication needs of a household. Prior to and during the concept development process, the team variously assessed stakeholder needs. They held group brainstorming sessions, did library research, kept home diaries of what unfilled needs they experienced themselves, and conducted extensive personal interviews with target customers. They also researched the technology that either was available at the time or would become so within the following two years.

Joining what they learned about customer needs and possible technologies to what they knew about the company's strategic plans, the team came up with a concept called "The Butler." The Butler was intended to present the image of a device that essentially would "take care of many repetitive and mundane tasks, and help organize and manage the home environment."[7] The concept also included details about the physical product (e.g., that it would include a base station and a portable unit arranged in a client-server relationship, and that there would be connections from the base unit to the electrical system, phone lines, and home appliances to allow for certain types of linkage). With this combination of the butler image and specific product features the team was able to move forward in the development process, using the same "script" to guide them in their decisions.

Concepts come from innumerable sources. Broadly, they can stem from an individual's inspirations or represent the output of a group assembled specifically to generate concepts. By and large, the benefit of the former source is that underlying the ideas of individuals are degrees of creativity and differentiation which are often suppressed in a group. The drawback is that the perspective of one person may not take into account all the important downstream issues surrounding the creation and distribution of a product. The more methodical group approach addresses this downstream problem but often at the expense of product uniqueness and distinction; reaching consensus can frequently arise only after the concept has been so chipped away it represents a bland compromise. If the product's *integrity* is kept in mind, this erosion may be prevented, however.

Product integrity refers to "the extent to which the totality of a product achieves the balance [of numerous product characteristics, including basic functions, aesthetics, semantics, reliability, and economy] and attracts and satisfies customers."[8] Integrity is a result of "internal" elements, such as how well the components of the system fit together or how efficient is its design, and "external" features, such as how well the product and its delivery system fit the needs of the customer. A weight machine available in many fitness centers, for example, may appear on the outside to be smooth and efficient, with its shiny metal, clean lines, and space-age appearance. If, however, the pieces underneath the glossy veneer have a bit of play in them, allowing them to slip slightly, the chains may start to rattle and the weight plates might begin to rub against each other. The result will be a clanging, friction-filled mess that does not support the smooth image presented by the exterior. The lack of internal integrity will have affected the external integrity as well, since some of the customer's needs – say, quiet workout, consistent measurement of amount of force exerted by user – remain unfulfilled.

---

[7] M, Bauer, T. Corn, S. Mertens, and M. Okuno, *The Butler: Contract Book* (written for Professor Marco Iansiti's "Managing Product Development" course, Harvard Business School, Spring 1994).

Product Architecture

An important aspect of the product concept affecting both internal and external product integrity is that of "product architecture," which refers to the physical building blocks or chunks assembled to create the whole unit. At one extreme, a product can be created as one entire block with no logical division except at the individual component level. Early mainframe computers employed this model. Every new product was basically an entirely new unit, and the company's customers essentially had to throw out the old one and buy the new. Development lead times were typically long, since the whole product was totally redesigned and reconfigured. Alternatively, the use of modules or separable chunks fit together with well-defined interfaces has become increasingly more popular in product design. The benefits of such a construct are many: parts of the product can be upgraded or fixed easily without affecting the rest of the system; new versions can be introduced to the market frequently; and often the risk of encountering technological problems when bringing out new products can be lessened since the development and debugging can be performed incrementally. Personal computers follow this model. If a user wants to improve his display capabilities or increase his system's memory, he only has to buy a new display unit or replace memory chips, respectively, while keeping everything else the same. The potential drawback of a modular design is that the interfaces can reduce overall product performance. In the case of the personal computer, in order to allow a unit to work with various operating systems (modularizing the operating system), the processor's full capability may not be utilized since it has to be general enough to run with various vendors' products. However, the typical PC user is willing to accept the drawbacks in order to gain the price and upgradability advantages the modular system provides.

Factors that weigh heavily in determining how modular to make a product include: how often the product needs to be changed (e.g., upgrades, add-ons, wear-and-tear replacements), how many different varieties of the same basic unit are desired, what level of performance the system must achieve (flexibility sometimes comes at the expense of performance should the pieces not fit together as perfectly as they could be when designed as an integral unit), and manufacturability and design (is it easier to assign design responsibilities by module or to purchase an entire module from a third party?).

Concept Selection

Once generated, concepts need to be evaluated and pared down. Their evaluation might lead to the discovery of more concepts (either by coming up with a new one while examining a previously one, or by combining already proposed ideas). The list will likely go through streamlining, slight expansion, then more narrowing, until a handful of "finalists" has been selected. There are no hard and fast rules for how the final concept should be selected, but the intent should be to devise the best *overall* solution given the relative and absolute importance ratings of stakeholder needs and company exigencies. Succinctly, the final concept should be checked for internal and external product integrity. Because some ultimate measures of the product's success may not be quantifiable, the qualitative nature of this screening process should be taken seriously. The benefits of having spent enough time up front to truly understand stakeholder needs in a general sense are very apparent at this point. Such understanding will help the team choose among the multiple desirable concepts to find the real winner.

One method that is frequently used to screen product concepts is conjoint analysis(see **Appendix B** for a description of this technique). In a nutshell, conjoint analysis allows product development teams to ask potential customers to rank alternative concepts, and then uses computer-based modeling to estimate the importance of various product features, and the potential market share that might be captured by alternative concepts. Conjoint analysis has been used extensively

---

[8] Ibid.

by manufacturing companies, market research firms, and even strategy consulting firms at the early stage of the product development process to assess the relative merits of different concepts before heavy investments are made in any of them.

Product Engineering and Design

Unhappily, a good concept alone does not ensure success. A good concept will only result in a good product if it is effectively translated into a detailed design with coherence and integrity. Countless products from the 1980s and 1990s have demonstrated that good design can have a tremendous impact on the success of a product. Chrysler, now considered one of the hottest automobile manufacturers in the world, can attribute much of its success to the creative and well-executed design of its products, such as the LH sedan and the recently introduced Neon. In the Neon, for example, a playful cartoon-like product concept was represented coherently through many details, from the sound of the engine to the shape of the door handles. The Apple Powerbook, whose sales greatly exceeded expectations, owed much of its appeal to the functionality and integrity of its design, from the innovative track-ball to the palm rest configuration. Oxo, a small manufacturer of kitchen utensils, owed its rapid growth to its revolutionary handle design. Its "big grip" products were able to earn a premium in a previously price-sensitive market. The field of industrial design has played a significant role in these success stories by emphasizing customer focus, creativity, integrity, and attention to detail.

To many people, engineering refers to the "guts" or insides of a product while design applies to that which is visible. While it is true that designers tend to have more of an impact on the appearance of a product, and the engineers might be more involved in the configuration of its parts, the lines of differentiation are not nearly so precise. Designers at an automobile company, for example, will be involved in creating both the exterior shape of the car and the cooling system hidden beneath it. Similarly, the engineers at a camera company might spend most of their time looking at the film winding mechanism in the camera, but they would also be involved in making decisions about parts that interface with the product users. In all situations, engineers and designers have the goal of determining how to match the needs, or design parameters, provided by the internal customers (e.g., manufacturing, shipping, service) to those of the external customers that were uncovered through the customer needs activities described earlier.

A glimpse of what designers and engineers do is offered by a group of Harvard Business School students.[9] Working with Kodak to expand its Photo CD product line,[10] the students uncovered a set of customer needs through interviews and surveys, and used those needs to arrive at a concept they recommended Kodak pursue further (see **Exhibit 1** for concept drawings). The team added more detail to the concept and came up with drawings like those in **Exhibits 2a** and **2b**. The next step for the team was to work with Kodak designers to bring the pictures to life in some non-functioning prototypes fabricated by Kodak's model shop (see **Exhibits 3a** and **3b**). Although these exhibits depict the product's exterior, the students bringing the engineers' perspectives to the process were involved in their creation as well; questions of how big to make the casing and how sharply the corners could slope, for example, could only be answered by looking at what was to be contained within the casing and in what configuration. Through an iterative process, the inside and the outside pieces were adjusted until they fit together in the optimal configuration.

---

[9] W.S. Bennet, W.C. Bennet, K.L. Hoernlein, P.L. Rice, D.G. O'Connor, S.M. Salzinger, and R.I. Webber, *Kodak Photo CD/Computer Product: Contract Book* (written for Professor Marco Iansiti's "Managing Product Development" course, Harvard Business School, Spring 1994).

[10] A Photo CD is a compact disc that stores photographs. When put into a Photo CD reader (or a CD-ROM drive with appropriate software), the photos can be displayed on a television monitor or manipulated on the computer.

Prototyping

Prototypes are representations of all or a portion of a product; they are created during the development process to accommodate any one of a handful of purposes. The completeness of the prototype varies according to how far along in the process it is created and what purpose it intends to serve. Typically, prototypes are used to meet one or more of the following goals:

1) *Test the feasibility of a concept* – this can be done either through physical or analytical (computer, mathematical) modeling.

   For example: Do the pieces fit together well? Can they be built that way at a low enough cost? If built as designed, will the motor make too much noise or is it properly insulated?

2) *Collect customer/stakeholder feedback on part or all of the concept.*

   For example: Does the unit feel comfortable in the user's hand? Is it sturdy enough that when packed sufficiently, it will arrive at the retailer unbroken?

3) *Communicate an idea (to other members of the company, suppliers, distributors, and so forth).*

   For example: When trying to get management to invest more money so that a particular concept can be pursued rather than the cheaper one, it is helpful to show the differences between the two.

Knowing why a prototype is being created is an important first step toward having it provide its intended benefits. In addition to identifying the purpose, however, questions about how accurate and complete the prototype should be need to be answered. A small appliance manufacturer wanted to make sure, before it ordered molds, that the newly designed blender would not overheat when run through reliability testing. To avoid incurring the expense of having just one molded unit built, engineers used an existing unit with the same dimensions but of a slightly different shape to run the tests. The motor did heat up but was about 5% below the allowed maximum, and the molds were ordered as a result. When actual tests were run on the first blenders made from production parts, however, the units heated up to 5% *above* the maximum. The team had made the mistake of not realizing how accurate the prototypes needed to be or what range of results would be acceptable given the slightly different parts it was using.

Also at issue in the development of prototypes is who should be involved in their construction and testing. Quite often, the functional area directly affected by the results performs the tests. In the blender case, the most salient issue being investigated was technical performance, and therefore the engineers built the prototypes and performed initial tests. Later in the process, as esthetic features became more important, marketing and industrial designers did prototype work. In this arrangement, little information about one series of tests spread throughout the organization so that everyone could know what was being learned. As a result, subsequent tests or decisions made by members of the development team not present for the building and testing done earlier failed to incorporate the information already gathered.

Pilot Production and Ramp Up and Market Launch

As suggested in the example above, prototypes are often used throughout the development process to prove the manufacturability of a particular design. If prototyping has been effective, therefore, by the time the final design has been accepted the factory should be nearly ready to execute full-scale production. This final move toward commercial production entails three steps: pilot production, ramp up, and market launch.

Pilot production is the stage at which a factory first uses parts produced by the molds, machines, and suppliers that will ultimately be employed when the products are being shipped to customers. The purpose is to test the notion that the company is ready to ship the product to customers, and the goal is to confirm the assembly, test, and other operational procedures used in full-scale production. All parts suppliers should be ready to support anticipated levels of production, and all equipment should be in place in the factory.

Once the basic process has been established, the manufacturing facility needs to develop the capability to produce the volume of units that are expected within the first year or so. The phase is termed "ramp up" since the increase is generally gradual, rather than in the form of a step function. This should be a learning and adjusting period for all those concerned (manufacturing, design, suppliers, shipping, and so forth) since increased volumes typically reveal problems that have not appeared previously.

Market launch is the phase in which the marketing plans regarding the target segment, positioning, product and service combinations, pricing, marketing communications, and distribution are executed in an integrated way to ensure the right product gets to the right customers at the right time for the right price.

At this point, the success of the development process can begin to be gauged. The Stage-Gate Model calls this the Post-Implementation Review. If the process was performed properly, manufacturing ramp up should be short and lacking major surprises (although inevitably there are some problems), the product should begin to flow through the distribution channels, and the anticipated demand should become visible. As with any other experience, however, the procedure should not be considered complete until an analysis of what went well and not-so-well during the development process has been performed and the relevant lessons taught throughout the organization.

References

Bowen, H.K., Clark, K.B., Holloway, C.A., and Wheelwright, S.C. (Eds.) *The Perpetual Enterprise Machine*, New York: Oxford University Press, 1994.

Clark, K.B., and Fujimoto, T. *Product Development Performance*, Boston, MA: HBS Press, 1991.

Clausing, D. *Total Quality Development*, 1994.

Cooper, R.G. "Stage-Gate Systems: A New Tool For Managing New Products," *Business Horizons*, May-June 1990, pp. 44-54.

Dolan, R.J. *Managing the New Product Development Process: Cases and Notes*, Reading, MA: Addison-Wesley, 1993.

Ulrich, K.T., and Eppinger, S.D. *Methodologies for Product Design and Development*, New York: McGraw-Hill, 1994.

Von Hippel, E. *The Sources of Innovation*, New York: Oxford University Press, 1988.

Wheelwright, S.C., and Clark, K.B. *Revolutionizing Product Development*, New York: The Free Press, 1992.

Appendix A: The Kano Method

The Kano Method recognizes that the degree of fulfillment of a customer requirement does not always correlate in one predictable manner with the level of customer satisfaction. In other words, the relationship between fulfillment and satisfaction is not always the same nor is it always linear. For instance, every increase in horsepower for a new car might not give the customer the same increase in happiness. Moving from 100 to 150 horsepower might be a big improvement in the customer's eyes, but a move from 300 to 350 may not be quite so important if 300 hp were more than enough for the target customer base. This is an example of a non-linear attribute. **Figure A1** displays qualitatively a few of the different relationships that can exist between the fulfillment of a need and the degree of customer satisfaction. A "delighter" is one that can only have positive customer satisfaction; its absence does not lead to customer dissatisfaction (i.e. , a point below the x-axis). On the other hand, a "must have" will never make a customer happy. It is expected that the product have the feature, so the best that a development team can hope to do is find out how much of the feature (how far to the right on the x-axis) the product should have so the customer will not be dissatisfied. (**Figure A1**, a qualitative visual tool, is not meant to indicate any precise or measurable relationships.)

Figure A1: The Kano Method

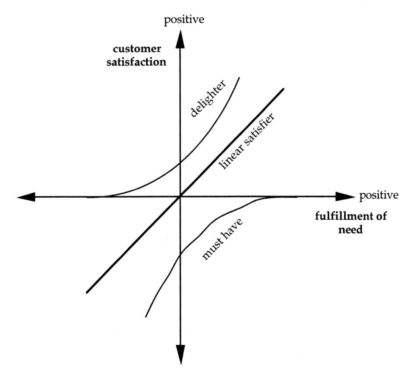

The Kano method is frequently implemented through a customer questionnaire. Two questions, one positive and one negative, are included for each customer need. For example, if a user need for a new mountain bike were that the rear tire should be easy to change, the positive question would read: "If the rear tire is easy to change, how do you feel?" while the negative one would ask, "If the rear tire is not easy to change, how do you feel?" For each question, the respondent is given five options: "I like it that way," "It must be that way," "I am neutral," "I can live with it that way," "I dislike it that way." The responses are processed by using a "two-dimensional table of evaluation" (see **Figure A2**) to translate them into the different labels.

Figure A2: Kano Method Evaluation Table

Result of Negative Question

	Like	Must Be	Neutral	Live with	Dislike
Like	Q	D	D	D	L
Must Be	R	I	I	I	M
Neutral	R	I	I	I	M
Live With	R	I	I	I	M
Dislike	R	R	R	R	Q

Result of Positive Question

I = Indifferent   M = Must Have
R = Reverse   L = Linear Satisfier
Q = Questionable Result   D = Delighter

Adapted from G. Burchill. *Concept Engineering: An Investigation of TIME vs. MARKET Orientation in Product Concept Development*, 1993.

The labels respondents assign must be summarized for each need before they can be used in the design process. Ideally, one summary label would be attached to each need based on the responses. For example, if one feeling predominates (e.g., 70% of respondents consider a particular need to be "must have"), that label can be assigned to the need. If, however, there is less harmony among the various respondents (e.g. 40% see it as "must have," 35% as "linear satisfier," 15% as "indifferent," and 10% as "reverse"), assigning one label would misrepresent the level of agreement between customers. In this case, instead of simply keeping one label attached to the user need, it might be better if the percentages for each label were recorded for those particular needs.

Once summarized for each need, the labels can be used to prioritize product requirements during the design process. Most development projects involve tradeoffs among product requirements. If, for example, both "make the rear tire easy to change" and "make the bike light" were customer requirements, the team might be confused about whether to improve the ease of changing the rear tire should doing so make the bicycle heavier. The decision might be easier if the development team knew that 60% of the respondents thought the lightness of the bike was a "must have" (assuming the definition of "light" has been clarified), while only 20% of the respondents thought the ease of changing the rear tire was a "must have." This information would indicate to the team that it should make the rear tire easier to change only if it did not negatively affect the weight of the bike.

Appendix B: Conjoint Analysis

Another technique that can be used to evaluate concepts during new product development is conjoint analysis. This technique requires more quantitative analysis by the new product development team than Kano Analysis; however, like Kano Analysis, it is relatively simple for potential customers to express their preferences. Here's an example of how it works:

First, a potential customer is shown a set of descriptions of alternative product concepts. The concepts are typically verbal descriptions of between three and seven product attributes. For example, imagine that you have been asked to participate in a market research study about how customers choose automobile tires. The market researcher asks you to rank from 1 (most preferred) to 6 (least preferred) the concepts below:

A Goodyear Aquatred brand tire, with guaranteed tread life of 80,000 miles, a price of $90 per tire, and a tire store that is a 30-minute drive from your home.

A Michelin brand tire, with guaranteed tread life of 80,000 miles, a price of $110 per tire, and a tire store that is a 10 minute drive from your home.

A private label tire, with guaranteed tread life of 60,000 miles, a price of $70 per tire, and a tire store that is a 30 minute drive from your home.

A Goodyear Aquatred brand tire, with guaranteed tread life of 60,000 miles, a price of $110 per tire, and a tire store that is a 10-minute drive from your home.

A private label tire, with guaranteed tread life of 80,000 miles, a price of $70 per tire, and a tire store that is a 10 minute drive from your home.

A Michelin brand tire, with guaranteed tread life of 60,000 miles, a price of $90 per tire, and a tire store that is a 30 minute drive from your home.

By ranking these six concepts and six to twelve others like them, customers can provide the researcher with the ability to pinpoint the relative value each customer places on the different brand names, levels of guaranteed tread life, prices, and driving time to the store. Conjoint analysis uses a variation of regression analysis to estimate each customer's relative utility for different attributes based on a simple ranking of the product concepts, which are bundles of attributes.

For example, a conjoint analysis software program might generate a customer's utility scores for various product attributes, like the ones shown in **Figure B1**. The researcher would then be able to identify several things: (1) how much a customer valued moving from a price of $110 to $90, and from $90 to $70; (2) the relative value of the Goodyear Aquatred and the Michelin brands compared to a private label; and (3) by calculating the difference between the lowest and highest utility score for each attribute, the researcher can discern whether brand name is more important than price, or whether number of warranty miles is more highly valued than the driving time from a customer's home. For example, the customer in **Figure B1** places less importance on driving time than on guarantees (within the ranges tested), because the difference in utility for 10 minutes versus 30 minutes is less than the difference in utility between a 60,000 and 80,000 mile guarantee.

Figure B1: Example of Conjoint Analysis Results for a Single Customer

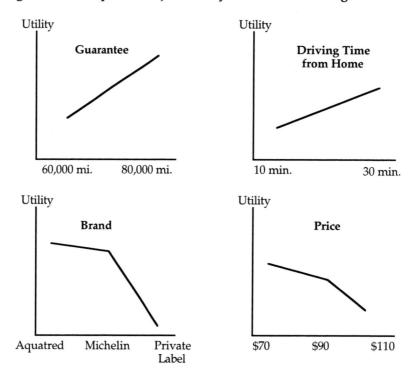

Because a customer's ranking of the alternatives may be similar to or different from those of other customers, the utilities of those customer may also be very similar or very different. Customers with similar utility scores can be grouped in the same "benefits segment." They value the same benefits, and can be satisfied with the same product-service-price bundle. Customers with different utility scores form different market segments that might be better served with different product-price-service combinations. Thus, another key benefit of conjoint analysis is that a product development team can estimate the share of market that a product concept would capture if it were launched under different scenarios, against different sets of products from competitors. This allows a product development team at the early stages of the NPD process to eliminate concepts with low market share potential before making the investment in building a prototype.

Conjoint analysis involves five choices by the researcher: (1) how to determine the relevant attributes; (2) how to show and describe the product concepts to customers (e.g., word descriptions versus words and pictures); (3) how to ask for the customers reactions (e.g., ranking concepts versus making tradeoffs between two attributes); (4) what customer decision criterion to use (e.g., asking which alternatives customers most prefer versus which ones they are most likely to buy) and (5) how to analyze the data (e.g.; simple regression versus MONANOVA – a regression-like technique for use with rank order data).[11]

In summary, conjoint analysis is a widely-used quantitative tool which, if employed correctly, provides reliable information about customer preferences that can be aggregated across customers into forecasts of market share for alternative new product concepts to customers in different benefit segments.

---

[11] See Dolan, *Managing the New Product Development Process*, pp. 115-119.

Product Development: A Customer Driven Approach

Exhibit 1 Concept Drawing of a Kodak Photo CD Read/Write Unit

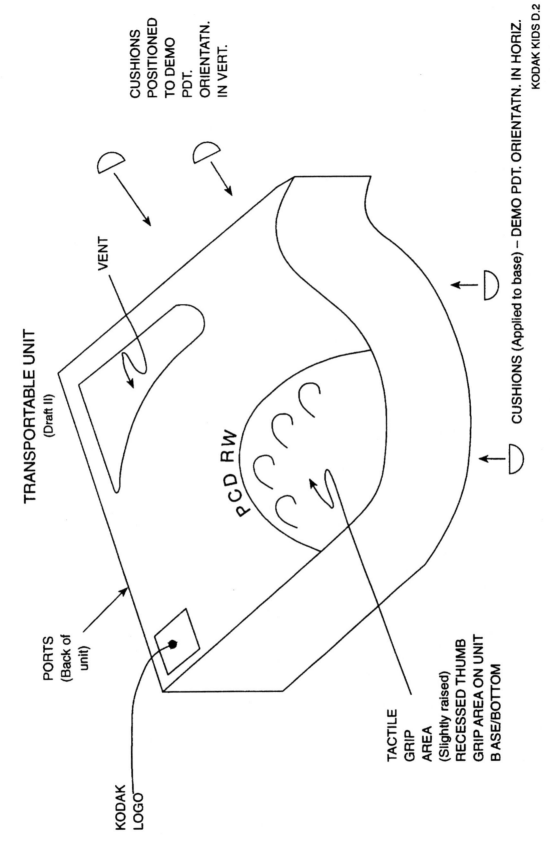

Compliments of Wendy and Stiles Bennet, Kurt Hoernlein, Patti Rice, Diane O'Connor, Steve Salzinger, and Rob Webber, MBA 1994, for the "Managing Product Development" course.

Exhibit 2a Engineering Drawing of a Kodak Photo CD Read/Write Unit

TOP

WALL THICKNESS:
.080 - .100"

RADIUS CORNERS:
.025"

*DRAWING DOES
NOT INCLUDE
RAISED GRIP
AREA

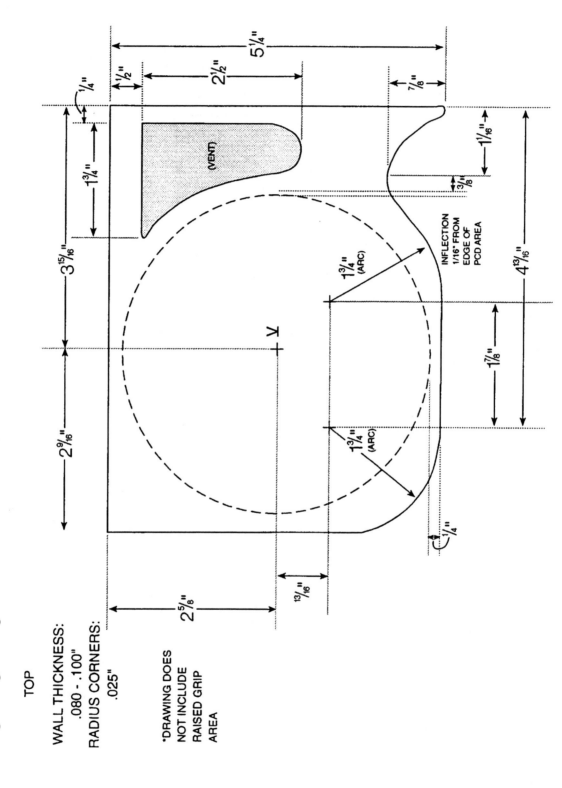

KODAK KIDS D.2

Compliments of Wendy and Stiles Bennet, Kurt Hoernlein, Patti Rice, Diane O'Connor, Steve Salzinger, and Rob Webber, MBA 1994, for the "Managing Product Development" course.

Product Development: A Customer Driven Approach

Exhibit 2b Engineering Drawing of a Kodak Photo CD Read/Write Unit

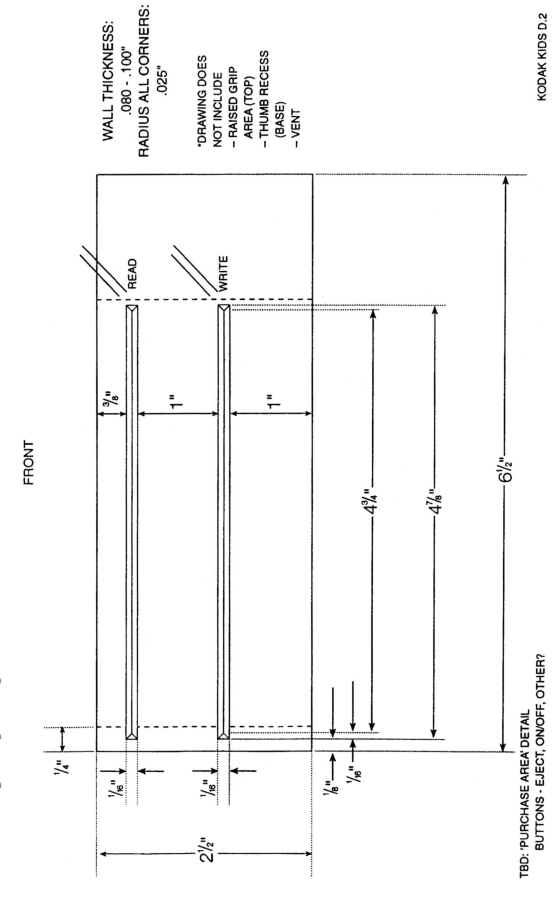

FRONT

WALL THICKNESS:
.080 - .100"
RADIUS ALL CORNERS:
.025"

*DRAWING DOES
NOT INCLUDE
- RAISED GRIP
  AREA (TOP)
- THUMB RECESS
  (BASE)
- VENT

READ

WRITE

$\frac{3}{8}$"

1"

1"

$\frac{1}{4}$"

$\frac{1}{16}$"

$\frac{1}{16}$"

$\frac{1}{8}$"

$\frac{1}{16}$"

$2\frac{1}{2}$"

$4\frac{3}{4}$"

$4\frac{7}{8}$"

$6\frac{1}{2}$"

TBD: 'PURCHASE AREA' DETAIL
BUTTONS - EJECT, ON/OFF, OTHER?

KODAK KIDS D.2

Compliments of Wendy and Stiles Bennet, Kurt Hoernlein, Patti Rice, Diane O'Connor, Steve Salzinger, and Rob Webber, MBA 1994, for the "Managing Product Development" course.

Exhibit 3 Non-Functional Prototype of a Kodak Photo CD Read/Write Unit

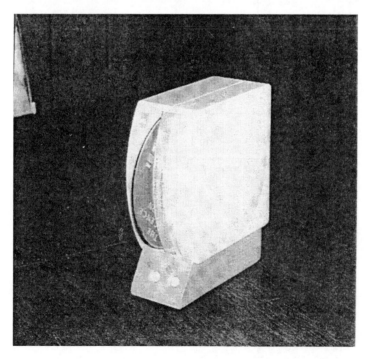

The work was based on drawings by Wendy and Stiles Bennet, Kurt Hoernlein, Patti Rice, Diane O'Connor, Steve Salzinger, and Rob Webber, MBA'94, for the *Managing Product Development* course.

NOTE ON LEAD USER RESEARCH

(S. Thomke / #9-699-014 / 12 p)

Summary

The author describes the lead user concept and outlines a step-by-step method for conducting lead user research.

Outline

Who Are Lead Users?
Lead User Research Methodology
Conducting a Lead User Study
Stage I: Project Planning (4-6 weeks)
Stage II: Trends/Needs Identification (5-6 weeks)
Stage III: Preliminary Concept Generation (5-6 weeks)
Stage IV: Final Concept Generation (5-6 weeks)
After the Project: Testing the Concepts

Learning Objectives

- Understand who lead users are and what role they can play in new product development
- Identify potential lead users for a new product
- Begin to plan a lead user study
- Use specific criteria to identify the best colleagues to participate on a lead user study team

Questions, Ideas, and Exercises

1. The author identifies three types of lead users:
- Lead users in the target application;
- Lead users in analogous markets;
- Lead users involved with attributes of problems faced by users in the target market.

Consider one of your company's products. With a colleague, brainstorm some possible uses or applications of this product by these three types of lead users. Which new applications are likely to be supported by senior management? Which fit with your firm's strategy and financial constraints? What resources would you need to consult to further refine this list?

2. The author lists several criteria that managers can use when forming a lead user research team. Use these criteria to begin to identify candidates for a lead user study. You might consider the following questions:

- Which colleagues know the most about the type of product you want to develop?
- Which colleagues are either seasoned team participants or likely to work effectively on a team?
- Which colleagues would be willing and able to contribute up to one-third of their time to this project? What arrangements are necessary in order to make this happen?

3. Take a look at Exhibit 3, "Major Lead User Research Activities and Suggested Time Allocations." With a colleague, use this chart to begin to map a lead user project that would be based on your work in the preceding exercises. Be sure to do the following:
- Make a preliminary assessment of the people and resources necessary to complete each stage.
- Plan how you and your colleagues will incorporate the lead user project into your current workload.
- Decide what steps you will take to gain the support of senior management.

Note on Lead User Research[1]

Jim Sanchez, a Bose Speakers Professional Products manager with responsibility for developing new products, was pleasantly surprised by the high quality of the background music he heard when he walked into a Boston-area Strawberries, a local chain of CD stores. On investigation he found that the manager had bought several Bose speakers designed for home use and asked electricians to install them "somehow." At that time, in the late 1980s, none of the available speakers were designed for mounting from above, but an electrician had wrapped metal straps around the speaker boxes to suspend them over people's heads — not necessarily safely. Sanchez went back to his office with Polaroid pictures of some of the improvised installations. Bose engineers quickly built prototypes, which they took back to Strawberries for further testing. This serendipitous discovery of a "lead user" need led Bose to successfully pioneer high fidelity speakers for the background music market.[2]

Who are Lead Users?

Most people are familiar with the concept of lead users at an intuitive level. Many customer products have, after all, been developed by lead users. The prototype for protein-based hair conditioners, for instance, came from daring women in the 1950s who experimented with home-made concoctions containing beer or eggs to impart more body and shine. Familiar consumer products ranging from Gatorade to graham cracker crust to sport bras to mountain bikes to surf boards all stem from consumer ideas and innovations.

For any market or product, there will almost always be individuals who experience needs ahead of everyone else. An intuitive notion of lead users based on the above examples, however, can prove misleading. Lead users are not necessarily recognized "opinion leaders" in a field. Rather, they lead with respect to cutting-edge applications of important market and technical trends. They

---

[1] Much of the information comes from E. von Hippel, J. Churchill, M. Sonnack, *Breakthrough Products and Services with Lead User Research* (Cambridge, Mass. and Minneapolis, Minn.: Lead User Concepts, Inc., 1998, forthcoming Oxford University Press).

[2] For a fuller account of this example, see E. von Hippel, J. Churchill, M. Sonnack, *Breakthrough Products and Services with Lead User Research*, page 1:20-1:21.

Professor Stefan Thomke and Research Associate Ashok Nimgade, M.D., prepared this case as the basis for class discussion rather than to illustrate either effective or ineffective handling of an administrative situation.

generally experience needs *ahead* of the market segment in which they operate (see **Exhibit 1**). Three types of lead users exist:

1. Lead users in the *target* application. This may include lead users who have actually experimented with developing prototypes. The Strawberries CD chain store example provides a good illustration of this group of lead users.

2. Lead users in *analogous* markets — i.e., in fields with similar applications. For instance, a health care firm interested in antibacterial control products for humans might actually find a lead user from the veterinarian sciences.

3. Lead users involved with the more important *attributes* of problems faced by users in the target market. For instance, a refrigeration manufacturing firm may find lead users from the supercomputer industry, where cooling technology plays an important role in running the computers.

Obviously, a wealth of information pertaining to product development resides in lead users. Finding these people, however, is generally not easy. Casual surveys cannot always unearth them. Appropriate lead users may dwell upon untrodden ways, proving as elusive as Wordsworth's violet by a mossy stone "half-hidden from the eye." Even if one does find someone with the right technical background, that person may not prove the best communicator. One might end up sitting on a mother lode with no idea of how to extract anything of value.

Lead User Research Methodology

Lead User research, pioneered by Professor Eric von Hippel of the Massachusetts Institute of Technology (MIT), provides a means of accurately forecasting market opportunities by systematically tapping the expertise and experience base of lead users. The Lead User method, developed by von Hippel in conjunction with 3M scientist and internal consultant Mary Sonnack and organizational psychologist Joan Churchill, allows new product development to arise from a sensitive understanding of product features that, ideally, will matter most to customers several years later.

Several successful Lead User studies have helped corroborate the usefulness of Lead User methods in settings ranging from health care to telecommunications to food. With increasing experience in Lead User methodology, its benefits and challenges have become more apparent over time. The specific benefits of Lead User methods include:

*   Access to richer and more reliable information on emerging customer needs than can be provided through traditional marketing research. Lead User methods, however, complement, not replace, the need for traditional marketing research.

*   Development of better products and service concepts since these come out of better data on consumers' likely needs.

*   Acceleration of the product and service development process.

Specific challenges to successfully using the Lead User methodology also exist. These include:

*   Difficulty in predicting the pathway from start to finish. Because of the unexpected twists and turns projects take, the ultimate path followed may not be

obvious without the benefit of hindsight. At certain stages, therefore, financiers and divisional superiors can be left with sweaty palms.

- The high level of commitment needed in terms of quality and quantity of human resources. One study indicates that management in major U.S. firms commits only a small portion of the innovation budget for early market research and concept development.[3] The bias in most firms is to view the truly important work as commencing with formal product and process development.

- Difficulties in assessing any given individual's participation in a team-based effort. This can prove problematic for assessing royalties or promotions.

Conducting a Lead User Study

In the 1980s, a major food corporation identified two intersecting trends that seemed the most promising for developing a new snack food: a growing public interest in healthy foods and an interest in amateur or "weekend" athleticism. With this knowledge, they turned to Professor von Hippel for help. Thus was launched the "Olympic Snack" project, one of the earliest Lead User studies conducted.

Von Hippel and management consultant Lee Meadows launched a Lead User study with the intent of developing new healthy snack foods that would contribute to athletic performance. The two began the study by scanning sport magazines aimed at serious amateur athletes as well as research articles in sport nutrition. In their reading they found solid evidence linking some kinds of snacks to performance enhancement during and after athletic events. Satisfied that the project was feasible, they next conducted telephone interviews with elite athletes including Olympians, prominent coaches, and nutrition scientists. Through these interviews they identified a small group of innovative lead users that they felt could contribute to developing the "Olympic Snack." These lead users included an national medal-winning weight lifter, a nutrition scientist who had worked with an elite navy combat group, and a competitive bicycle racer.

It became apparent that knowledge about performance-enhancing foods was segmented between nutritionists and athletes. Nutritionists were more knowledgeable about what snacks should contain and how their consumption should be timed. They cared little about taste. The athletes, on the other hand, knew how snacks should be formulated for easy consumption in the midst of competition. Towards the end of the study, to focus on these two areas of knowledge, von Hippel and Meadows ran two different concept development workshops: one aimed at capturing the knowledge of the nutritionists and the other aimed at capturing the taste preferences of athletes. The combined knowledge from these workshops led to the development of concepts for a very novel line of healthy snacks.[4]

* * * * *

The Olympic Snack story illustrates how most Lead User projects work. The team typically begins with a little to a moderate amount of knowledge about the arena within which it expects to work. (Note that the Olympic Snack example is atypical in utilizing two external consultants rather than an inside team to conduct the entire study.) Initially the team must do its homework to develop a familiarity with the field. Thereafter, the study focuses on tapping unpublished knowledge that resides in leading-edge users and experts. Holding workshops with lead users toward the end of the

---

[3] R.G. Cooper, *Winning at New Products* (Reading, Mass.: Addison-Wesley Publishing Company, 1994).

[4] For a fuller account of this example, see E. von Hippel, J. Churchill, M. Sonnack, *Breakthrough Products and Services with Lead User Research* , page 1:16-1:17.

study allows the firm to capture what is hopefully the world's finest assemblage of living knowledge crucial to the particular product development. The entire process, while vigorous, stresses qualitative validity over statistical reliability — a feature that in an age of increasing quantification makes many market researchers queasy.

Lead User projects based within companies can take five or six months but gets faster with experience. During this time corporate team members involved spend 12 to 15 hours per week — or roughly up to a third of their time — on the project for its entire duration. This high level of immersion fosters creative thought and sustains project momentum. Lower levels of commitment, experience has shown, tend to make projects "drag on" and also bog down attempts to figure out where the team has left off.

As one might imagine, given the need for such commitment, the study's success relies heavily on selecting a talented core team and receiving strong support from senior management. Typically, a corporate team consists of four to six people, including representatives from marketing and technical departments, and requires about 12-15 hours per week of work. One or two members serve as project leaders. This team size appears to be large enough to generate diverse perspectives, yet small enough to facilitate team logistics and rapid team decision-making. Ideal team members have a deep and broad knowledge base relevant to the topic, remain open to new approaches, and enjoy thinking creatively.

In conducting a Lead User study, four stages can be defined (see also **Exhibits 2 and 3**). In reading descriptions of these stages below, it is useful to reflect on the Olympic Snack example.

Stage I: Project Planning (4-6 weeks)

This is essentially the "homework" or scouting phase of the study in which the team identifies types of markets and new products of interest it seeks to target. These markets and products, of course, should fit within the firm's key business goals and constraints. The team also seeks to define the desired level of innovation. For instance, does the company seek a "breakthrough" product or does it wish to merely extend current product or service lines?

At a tactical level, the team begins Stage I by getting "grounded" in the project, by reading trade journals, browsing through market surveys and market data, searching the Internet, or informally interviewing industry experts, who may include customers, suppliers, and internal company managers, to get a feel for current trends and market needs. Next, the group develops a specific data collection plan, focused on key questions (such as market trends) as well as key resources (appropriate experts and trade literature).

The challenge for most Lead User studies is to avoid downplaying the importance of this stage. The base of knowledge developed here will reap dividends down the road. According to Lead User process consultant Joan Churchill, "The lead user process is a very disciplined process. Teams that look for 'quick fixes' can end up disillusioned once they realize how much study is needed before getting to the 'fun stuff.' Teams that leapfrog the first stage by immediately starting to look for lead users may set themselves up for failure."[5]

---

[5] Interview with Joan Churchill, August, 1998.

Stage II: Trends/Needs Identification (5-6 weeks)

At this stage the team officially launches its Lead User study. The ultimate goal is to select a specific need-related trend(s) to focus upon for the remainder of the study. In the Olympic Snacks example, for instance, the team decided to address two intersecting trends involving a growing interest in healthy foods and an interest in amateur athleticism.

The team initiates the trend and market investigation with a focused, comprehensive trade literature review pertaining to the project. This helps provide a sense of the "conventional wisdom" relating to trends and market needs. Experience shows that a four-day team workshop provides the best way to kick off this stage. In the first two days of this session, members browse through reading material selected by the team during Stage I. Every two or three hours, group discussions cover what members are learning from the reading.

The next two days of this workshop lays the groundwork for interviewing lead users as well as lead use experts – individuals who, while not necessarily lead users, possess expertise relevant to lead use. In a half-day session, the team prepares an interview guide that covers key questions to explore with experts. The team spends another half-day conducting "warm-up" interviews with local experts. The reason for this heavy emphasis, as Churchill points out, is that, "Some technical people at corporations have never seen a customer face-to-face; and not many have good interviewing skills."[6]

The process of finding top experts involves querying industrial gurus, scanning literature, searching the Internet, and consulting with in-house colleagues. Telephone "networking" also helps identify appropriate experts. Interviewing typically takes place over the telephone, but it can also occur in person for certain experts with vital information.

Three or four weeks into Stage II, the team generally develops a good understanding of major trends and is now positioned for the vital task of "framing" the customer need that can be addressed by a new product or service. This needs-framing typically occurs through a series of meetings spread over two weeks, during which the team evaluates, interprets, and combines the data collected from readings and interviews.

Thereafter, teams typically take another two weeks to rework and refine initial ideas on needs-framing in light of further interviews and readings. This allows the team to zero in on the data directly pertaining to the project focus and set aside extraneous information.

Example:

Top executives at a company that manufactured hearing aids concluded that for their product development goals an ideal new product line would have several key features: it would yield profitability of $1-5 million in its first year, and over $20 million in later years. Furthermore, this product line would utilize existing company technologies and existing marketing channels. Instead of scouring the world — in manner of llamas seeking the next dalai lama — for products already born, the firm executives turned to a Lead User study.

To kick off the lead user project, 20 people from each of the firm's departments participated in a half-day brainstorming session. Of several product concepts discussed, the most promising was a low cost, quality hearing instrument to address the needs of people in their 50s suffering from early hearing loss. Current products on the market ignored the needs of this segment of the population.

---

[6] Ibid.

At the end of the brainstorming session, the team envisioned the new product line as being inexpensive (under $200), easy to use (with no need for adjustment by users or audiologists), and with significantly improved sound quality without acoustic feedback or background noise. Each early assumption about a product attribute led to new questions about which the team felt it had to learn more. Consider, the following:

- *Demographics: A rapidly growing number of people over 50 years old would suffer from mild to moderate hearing loss. New question: How many of these people are actually buying hearing aids? What features are they seeking?*

- *Product usage: The new product line would appeal to people in their 50s concerned with the cosmetics of hearing aids. New question: What cosmetic features would prove important to this population of aging "baby boomers?"*

- *Technology: Leading-edge products appear increasingly simple to use. New question: What new technologies in our own and other fields can help create easy-to-use, "one size fits all" type of hearing aids?*

After this "needs-framing" exercise, the team found itself ready to enter the next phase.[7]

Stage III: Preliminary Concept Generation (5-6 weeks)

With Stage III, all potential analogies to armchair philosophizing ends: The team now begins to generate preliminary concepts. First, however, the group must acquire a more precise understanding of the focal area. This understanding arises from the iterative process of seeking solutions to questions, which in turn generates further questions. The team continues interviewing lead user experts for technical knowledge that pertains to concept generation.

Many of the interviews occur at the lead user's own place of business. This provides invaluable information that the lead user might find commonplace and not worthwhile expressing, or information hard to explain over the telephone. (For instance, through annotated demonstrations like "At this point, I turn my home-crafted wood stake thus… before the vampire eludes my grasp.")

For concepts generated in this stage, the team must start outlining the attributes and features the ideal product should have, along with benefits and values offered to targeted customers and key design features. (Recall in the hearing aid example how the team addressed these key issues.) The team seeks to informally assess business potential for the product or service being conceptualized.

Toward the end of Stage III, the team meets with key managers responsible for implementing product development concepts that will ultimately rise from the Lead User project. By now, the team should be armed with some verifying evidence that the identified needs and preliminary solution ideas do indeed represent good business opportunities. This involves providing data on size and profitability of the targeted market as well as analysis of competitive offerings to make sure that preliminary concepts offer unique benefits and value to target customers.

Stage IV: Final Concept Generation (5-6 weeks)

In Stage IV, the team takes the preliminary concept developed in Stage III toward completion. Activity in this stage generally centers around a Lead User workshop of up to two or three days. The workshop serves to fill in missing pieces in the preliminary concepts developed in Stage III as well as

---

[7] For a fuller account of this example, see E. von Hippel, J. Churchill, M. Sonnack, *Breakthrough Products and Services with Lead User Research*, page 3:5-3:6.

to ensure that all possible solutions have been explored. During the workshop, the team works intensively with lead users and lead use experts to improve and add to the preliminary concepts.

Example:

A manufacturer of hardware products planning to develop abrasives for smooth surfaces that are difficult to sand down (e.g., banisters, chair legs, decorative moldings) ended up inviting to the workshop held during Stage IV lead users that included a designer of early American furniture, an internationally renown wood sculptor, and a specialist in guitar design and refurbishment. All these lead users were experts in the sanding of compound curves in wood (either by hand or under factory production conditions). Several design prototypes for viable products emerged from this confluence of diverse talents.[8]

A well-orchestrated workshop proves crucial for success. Typically, 15 to 18 people attend a Stage IV workshop, of which a third may come from the project team and from in-house technical or marketing divisions. The remaining attendees are lead users or lead use experts. While many of these may already have been identified in Stage II, further probing may be required to find people with appropriate expertise. Well over a month of planning may go into designing and scheduling the workshop.

At the very beginning of the workshop, which ideally is held off-site in pleasant surroundings, people take turns explaining their expertise and interests. The group then discusses the problem area and reviews background information. Because 15 to 18 people cannot discuss any matter efficiently, let alone civilly, much of the workshop occurs in subgroups, each of which discusses independent parts of the problem. Through the remainder of the workshop, these small groups are formed and re-formed for efficient cross-pollination of ideas and viewpoints.

Towards the end of the workshop, different subgroups are charged with generating alternative product concepts. Friendly rivalry between subgroups often spurs inventiveness and even the quest for increasingly novel solutions. Thereafter, the entire group meets to systematically evaluate the generated product concepts in terms of technical feasibility, market appeal, and management priorities. The entire group arrives at consensus on the most commercially promising concepts and develops recommendations for further steps to refine them. Here, the vast array of expertise allows for virtually instantaneous feedback. According to Rita Shor, a 3M product developer who led a Lead User study for developing surgical product concepts:

As concepts in our Lead User workshop were being developed, it was especially useful to get *immediate* feedback from the surgeons and microbiologists and skin bacteria specialists. Because of the high level of expertise and actual field experience that the external attendees brought to the workshop, the group generated ideas faster and explored them more deeply than would have been possible in one-to-one interviews.[9]

Obviously, the synergy from this meeting of minds provides one reason why most lead users and lead use experts are literally signing away intellectual property rights to innovations and product concepts that may stem from such workshops. Most invitees generally realize that on their own they may be unlikely to develop the particular innovations. Furthermore, many lead users and lead use experts enjoy contributing to innovations, even if only for the sake of innovation, and find such workshops intellectually stimulating. For some invitees, it provides a welcome change from an

---

[8] For a fuller account of this example, see E. von Hippel, J. Churchill, M. Sonnack, *Breakthrough Products and Services with Lead User Research*, page 4:18-4:19.

[9] E. von Hippel, J. Churchill, M. Sonnack, *Breakthrough Products and Services with Lead User Research*, p. 7:6.

intellectual isolation. Too many lead users, to return to Wordsworth, have remained like a solitary star in a sky.

Example:

For the hearing aid lead user workshop, the sponsoring firm had identified several key attributes that the ideal product should have. This made it easier to think about lead users the firm should invite for interviews and workshop attendance. As you read the list of desirable attributes below, you may think of yet more potential lead users and lead use experts than the firm identified.

- *Attribute 1 — cosmetic appeal: Lead uses/experts identified: cosmetic dentistry specialists; manufacturers of upscale costume jewelry.*

- *Attribute 2 — customizable low cost tubing: Lead uses/experts identified: medical tubing suppliers; manufacturers/suppliers of amplifiers for professional football teams.*

- *Attribute 3 — low acoustical feedback/minimal amplification of unwanted sound: Lead uses/experts identified: specialists in tiny circuitry and digital technology applications in the video and music industries.*

- *Attribute 4 — ease of purchase (without need for ear exams or special fittings): Lead uses/experts identified: opticians who had pioneered sales of contact lenses through mass retailers; major retailers that sold eyeglasses and offered on-site eye exams.*

Afterward, the team refines the preliminary concept on the basis of knowledge gained from the workshop with lead users and lead use experts who attended that meeting. The team presents senior managers with information about the proposed products or services, providing solid evidence about why customers would be willing to pay for them. Among the visual tools found useful for this meeting are sketches of the concepts and videotaped clips from the lead user workshop.

After the Project: Testing the Concepts

Since lead users are not the same as routine users in a target market, concepts should be tested on ordinary consumers in the target market. The nature of validation required varies from firm to firm, depending on how much commercial promise concept evaluators anticipate the concept to hold.

Quite often, quantitative methods for evaluating routine products do a poor job of evaluating the novel functions and benefits offered by "breakthrough" products and services. For this reason, many Lead User project managers evaluate concepts based on small groups of users in the target markets as well as on their own judgment. In some cases, however, because of considerations of secrecy, some firms have opted skip this testing on routine users.

At least one member of the lead user team should help shepherd the product or service concept through the next development phases to ensure that the expertise built through the entire process of the study is fully deployed. This also helps ensure that innovative products do not get tangled in a web of "business as usual" practices. For instance, after the Olympic Snack study, the sponsoring firm planned to test the new product line the way it tested all its other products: on housewives shopping in supermarkets. Only timely intervention from the lead user product champion steered testing toward the target market of weekend athletes.

* * * * *

Increasing experience with Lead User methodology over the years suggests that three elements are necessary for a successful study:

(1) *supportive management* that will provide the project the creditability and long-term commitment required;

(2) the use of a *cross-discipline Lead Use study team of highly skilled people* comprising the very best people with years of experience, creativity, and good team skills;

(3) a clear *understanding of the principles of Lead User research,* which may gain further from use of a consultant who can coach the process through the nuances of the method.

By its very nature, innovation remains an unpredictable process that does not lend itself to lockstep algorithms. The methods described above may provide a key to the successful courtship of the muse of innovation.

Exhibit 1   Position of Lead User Relative to Market

Characteristics of Lead Users

1. Lead users have new product or service needs that will be general in a marketplace, but they face them months or years before the bulk of the market encounters them.

2. Lead users expect to benefit significantly by finding a solution to their needs. As a result, they often develop new products or services themselves because they can't or don't want to wait for them to become available commercially.

3. Lead users are not the same as "early adopters" – users who are among the first people to purchase an existing product or service (see figure below). Lead users are facing needs for products and services that *do not exist* on the market.

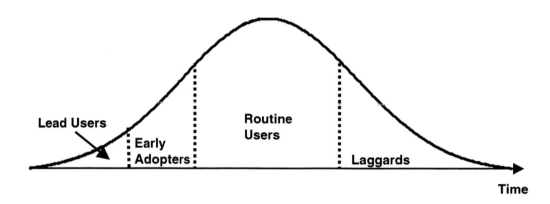

Exhibit 2   Summary of Lead User Research Process[10]

Stage 1: Preparing to Launch the Lead User Project

Key Management Activities

- Select the new product/service areas of interest.
- Designate a cross-disciplinary research team of 4-6 people to implement the project.

Key Team Activities

- Refine the focus through discussions with key stakeholders.
- Develop a data collection plan.

Stage 2: Identifying Trends and Key Customer Needs

Key Team Activities

- Broadly explore trends through interviews with lead use experts and reading in the trade literature.
- Select the markets and core needs that will be the focus of concept development.

Stage 3: Explore Lead User Needs and Solutions

Key Team Activities

- Generate preliminary solution concepts by interviewing lead users and lead use experts.
- Collect market data for a business case.
- Present needs data and preliminary solutions to management.

Stage 4: Improve Solution Concepts with Lead Users and Experts

Key Team Activities

- Hold a 2-3 day workshop to further develop concepts.
- Finalize concepts and develop a written new product or service proposal.
- Review the project output with management.

After the Workshop

- Test appeal of the concept(s) on target market(s).
- Hand-off the concept(s) for commercialization.

---

[10] E. von Hippel, J. Churchill, M. Sonnack, *Breakthrough Products and Services with Lead User Research* , page 2:21.

Exhibit 3   Major Lead User Research Activities and Suggested Time Allocations[11]

Stage/Major Activities	Who	Suggested Time by Activity
Stage 1: Project Planning • Develop master plan. • Learn about the current marketplace. • Further refine the project focus.	Project planners Project team	**4-6 weeks total** 10+ hrs. (over 1 month) 3-4 weeks
Stage 2: Trends/Needs Identification • Conduct literature searches. • Interview top experts. • Interpret/analyze data/select specific needs to focus on.	Individual team members Whole project team	**5-6 weeks total** 10+ hrs. per week 1+ hr. (weekly meeting)
Stage 3: Preliminary Concept Generation • Interview lead users and experts. • Gather data for business case. • Define new product or service requirements, generate concepts.	Individual team members Whole project team	**5-6 weeks total** 10+ hrs. per week 1+ hr. (weekly meeting)
Stage 4: Final Concept Development • Plan lead user workshop. • Invite participants. • Hold workshop – improve concepts with lead user/experts. • Finalize concepts.	Individual members Whole project team	**5-6 weeks total** 10+ hrs. (over 2 weeks) 2-3 days (typical length of workshop) 2+ weeks 10+ hrs. (2-3 meetings)
Project Wrap-Up • Evaluate project outcomes. • Plan next commercialization steps.	Management/project team	**2-3 meetings** 10+ hrs. (2-3 meetings)
Approximate Length of Project: 5-6 Months (with increasing experience and team members who dedicate over 50% of their time, the duration of a study can be reduced)		

---

[11] E. von Hippel, J. Churchill, M. Sonnack, *Breakthrough Products and Services with Lead User Research*, page 3:9.

NEW PRODUCT COMMERCIALIZATION: COMMON MISTAKES

(V. K. Rangan / #9-594-127 / 13 p)

Summary

The author discusses the common mistakes made in new product development and launch. He shows how these mistakes occur when customers' and suppliers' perceptions of how innovative a product really is don't match and what managers can do to help prevent this misunderstanding.

Outline

Marketing Mistakes
  A Framework
  Breakthroughs and Incrementals
  Mistake #1
  Mistake #2
  Shadowed New Products
  Mistake #3
  Delusionary New Products
  Mistake #4
Conclusions

Learning Objectives

- Understand why it is important to match the product development process to product type
- Understand the differences between incremental and breakthrough products
- Identify an incremental product that might be repositioned as a breakthrough, and begin to take steps to effect this change
- Evaluate their current product offerings in terms of their opportunity costs and development risks

Questions, Ideas, and Exercises

1. The author notes that the most common mistake in the new-product development process is "lack of sensitivity to the differences in the management tasks required of incremental versus breakthrough products." Think about a new product for which your company is going to assemble a cross-functional team. Does this new product represent a breakthrough or is it an incremental innovation?
- If a breakthrough, identify colleagues from marketing and manufacturing who are able to envision this product and how it will be used. What other colleagues are essential to balance the team?

- If an incremental innovation, identify colleagues from production and sales who are able to provide reliable customer data and cost estimates for this new product. What other colleagues are essential to balance this team?

2. Consider the product you focused on above. List the steps you will need to take to win top management's support for this development project. Be sure to identify:
- How the new product or service aligns with your firm's strategic objectives
- What its market potential is
- Whether it will require significant upfront investment or investment that is staged
- Colleagues from other departments whose support is essential to winning top management's approval.

3. Figure 2 shows how to match development process to type of product. Briefly list several new-product concepts that will soon enter the development process in your unit. Plot each on Figure 2 according to its opportunity cost and development risk. Are your new products clustered at one corner, or are they spread throughout the figure? What implications do these patterns have for how you can most effectively deploy your development resources?

4. Consider a product that you are currently marketing as an incremental innovation. With a colleague, identify two or three new customer segments that might view the product as breakthrough rather than incremental. Describe how the existing channel for this product would need to be reconfigured to reach these new customers. In particular, what opportunities exist to market or sell this product via the Web? Describe why and how you would change the pricing structure for customers in these new segments.

New Product Commercialization: Common Mistakes

It is widely acknowledged that a constant supply of new products and their successful commercialization are key to a firm's survival. But studies by Booz Allen and others have found that after all the time, effort, and money spent in screening and developing new products, 50% to 67% of them fail in the commercialization process.[1] Why do so many new products fail? In some cases, the product development process is flawed to start with. In others, the product concept is very poorly backed by market research. In some others, it is the launch process and its execution that is at fault. In any case, the failure statistic highlights the need for close management attention to the new product development and commercialization process. As a noted expert[2] concluded, "If half of a factory's output ended up as defects, you'd shut the place down."

Various remedies have been offered for streamlining and improving the new product development process. The concept of creating a team comprising members from different functions is probably the single most widely accepted concept in accelerating new product development. Such a team is able to solve potential problems early in the development cycle and engender commitment more easily from all of the involved functions.[3] The need for a product champion or a project manager to coordinate the team has also been highly recommended.[4] The whole idea, of course, is to move the project along its various phases (see **Figure 1**) as smoothly and efficiently as possible.

---

[1]Booz Allen & Hamilton, Inc. (1982), *New Product Management for the 1980s*, New York: Booz Allen & Hamilton.

[2]Robert G. Cooper, "Flops: Too many new products fail. Here's why - and how to do better," *Business Week*, August 16, 1993.

[3]Many articles and books have been written on the subject. The following are representative: Hirotake Takeuchi and Ikujiro Nanaka, "The New Product Development Game," *Harvard Business Review*, January-February, 1986. Steven C. Wheelright and Kim B. Clark, *Revolutionizing Product Development*, Free Press, 1992, pp. 165-217. Preston G. Smith and Donald G. Reinertsen, *Developing Products in Half the Time*, Von Nostrand Reinhold, 1991, pp. 111-151.

[4]The new product literature is flooded with stories of product champions, from Tom West of the Eclipse project (Trace Kidder, *The Soul of a New Machine*, The Atlantic Monthly Press, 1982) to the dozens of fascinating protagonists in *Breakthroughs*, Mercury, 1993, by P. Ranaganath Nayak & John M. Ketteringham.

Professor V. Kasturi Rangan and MBA Candidate Kevin Bartus prepared this note as the basis for class discussion.

Figure 1   New Product Development Stages

1. Initial screening

The initial decision to go ahead with the project; the idea having been screened in from several alternatives.

2. Preliminary market assessment

The preliminary market study: a "quick and dirty" situation analysis of the marketplace, possible market acceptance and competitive assessment.

3. Preliminary technical assessment

An initial technical appraisal, addressing questions such as "can the product be developed? can it be manufactured?" etc.

4. Detailed market study

Marketing research: detailed market studies such as user needs-and-wants analysis, concept tests, positioning studies and competitive analyses.

5. Preliminary business analysis

Comprehensive business analysis with projected net present values, pro-forma income statements, etc.

6. Product development

The actual development of the physical product leading up to a prototype.

7. Alpha tests

Testing the product in-house under controlled or laboratory conditions.

8. Beta tests

Testing the product with customers field trials.

9. Test market

An attempt to sell the product to a limited market area or customers, to gauge product acceptance in a real market context.

10. Trial production

A limited trial, or batch production run, designed to prove production facilities.

11. Final business plan

A final business and financial analysis prior to launch.

12. Production ramp up

Full-scale production.

13. Market launch

The implementation of a comprehensive marketing plan.

Adapted from Robert G. Cooper, "Winning at New Products," Addison-Wesley, Reading, Massachusetts, 1993, p.29.

While the dedication of a cross-functional team under the leadership of a project manager/product champion is necessary, it is not sufficient to ensure new product success.[5] A careful matching of the product development process to the type of product is required. (See **Figure 2**.)

---

[5]For more on this, see E.W. Larson and David H. Gobeli, "Organizing for Product Development Projects," *Journal of Product Innovation Management*, Vol 5, 1988, 180-90.

Krubasik[6] suggests different processes for different product contexts. While they all have to systematically navigate the 13 stages of a new product's development and launch, different levels of formal management sign-offs and check-points are appropriate for the different new product contexts. When the development risks are high and the opportunity costs are low, it is not particularly advantageous to accelerate product development. Such a process could boost project expense and jeopardize product performance and cost. A carefully controlled transition across each stage may make sense. Popularly called the stage-gate system,[7] such a process involves staging the development over several "gates." The project may proceed to the next gate only if it clears certain well-specified hurdles. At the other extreme, when the development risk is low and opportunity costs are high, it is absolutely important to speed up the process. Several steps may have to run concurrently. Fortunately, the risks of development failure are also low. The hardest process to manage is when the risks as well as the opportunity costs are high. While technology and cost considerations will necessitate a carefully staged process, market considerations demand speed. The process has to carefully blend caution and aggression.

Figure 2 Matching Development Process to Product Type

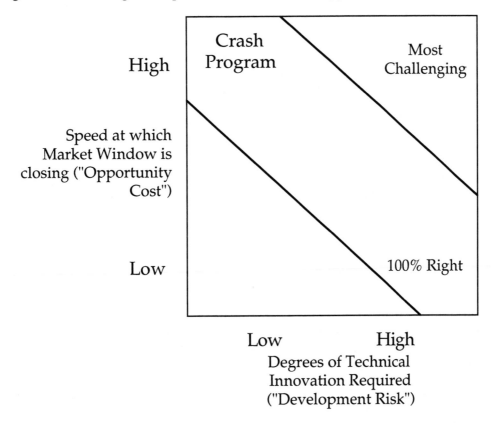

Source: Krubasik, Edward G., "Customize Your Product Development," HBR, Nov.-Dec., 1988

---

[6]Edward G. Krubasik, "Customize Your Product Development," *Harvard Business Review*, November- December, 1988.
[7]Robert G. Cooper, *Winning at New Products*, Addison-Wesley Publishing Company, 1993, pp. 95-120.

In summary, the new product literature offers us a wealth of guidelines on how to better manage the development and commercialization process, when to accelerate the steps, and how to effectively manage the teamwork. In this article, we focus on some common product-development and launch mistakes committed by firms that are fully cognizant of, and firmly committed to, the various prescriptions referred to above. Even though the problems we describe here are executional in nature, several of them are driven by a poor understanding of the development concept to start with.

Marketing Mistakes

A Framework

As shown in **Exhibit 1,** over the years many new product taxonomies have been offered. Products have been classified along various dimensions, such as newness of product/technology, newness to market, newness to company, extent of product change, extent of process change, etc. But curiously enough every one of these definitions assumes that the originator of the innovation and the customer are in complete agreement on the "newness" of the product or its "breakthrough" nature. But anecdotal evidence suggests that a significant number of new products fail precisely because suppliers and customers do not see eye-to-eye on what the product is supposed to do. There is a disjunction between the seller and the buyer. Consider the case of NeXT, a desktop computer developed by Steve Jobs, the legendary founder of Apple Computer.[8] Customers did not want the optical drive instead of the usual floppy drive. The new feature made it tough for them to switch work from a PC to NeXT. Even though the machine had other nifty features, such as hi-fi sound, customers never overcame their initial resistance. Students found it too expensive, while engineers thought that workstations delivered better performance and value. Thus, after spending $200 million to develop the product, Steve Jobs was forced to drop the product. Yet if he had listened to customers and gone with more standard technology earlier on, some analysts say he might have succeeded. The moral of the story is simple: the new product development process has to start with the voice of the customer,[9] and in this case the customers were seeking an incremental rather than a radical innovation. They were not prepared for the "next generation" product. They did not see the need for it, nor were they willing to pay for it.

In order to understand such supplier-customer misperceptions, we offer a framework to diagnose the problem. (See **Figure 3.**) On one axis we map the supplier's perception of the new product, and the customer's on the other. For simplicity, we divide the world into "breakthrough" inventions and "incremental" innovations, knowing full well that many intermediate positions are feasible. "Breakthrough" is an idea that is so different that it cannot be compared to any existing practices or perceptions. It employs a new technology and creates a new market. Breakthroughs are conceptual shifts that make history.[10] Incremental innovations on the other hand are continuations of existing methods or practices. Both suppliers and customers have a clear conceptualization of the product and what it can do. Existing products are sufficiently close substitutes.

---

[8]Adapted from *Business Week*, August 16, 1993, "Flops: Too many new products fail. Here's why - and how to do better."

[9]Vincent P. Barabba and Gerald Zaltman, *Hearing the Voice of the Market*, Harvard Business School Press, 1991, pp. 19-35.

[10]P. Ranaganath Nayak & John M. Ketteringham, *Breakthroughs*, Mercury, 1993, pp. 1.

When both the supplier and the customer view the new product context as a breakthrough, or as incremental, we then have the perfect match running from east to west in **Figure 3.** The mismatch is represented by the north-south axis.

Breakthroughs and Incrementals

Breakthrough products require intensive technology and/or applications development. Customers are awed by the new product's potential. It is often doubtful at this stage if a large number of customers really understand how the product usage characteristics will evolve and what usage patterns it will involve. It is important to have a technology vision at this stage in anticipation of market development. While a few "opinion-leader" type customers may share that vision, most customers may not have a clue. It would be futile, for example, to seek extensive customer opinion on product attributes and features because the product concept may appear too distant to be of immediate use. A bulk of the product development work, therefore, has to be undertaken with input from only a handful of customers. The effort is typically an "inside out" process, with the technology people playing an important role. Referred to as "empathic design," a projective vision and a keen sense of market anticipation is required in the product development process.[11]

Figure 3   New Product Types

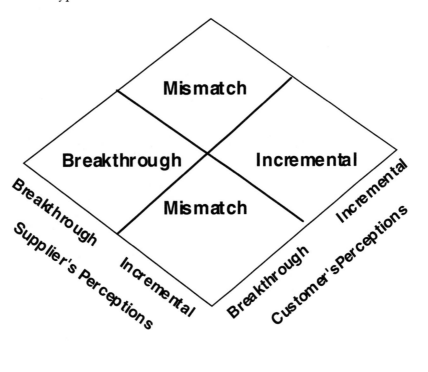

In sharp contrast, customers will be able to play a major role in providing input for incremental products. These are typically evolutionary development from their viewpoint. Based on their own product-usage history, customers usually will have a precise definition of what improvements they need in the product. Because of their experiences in making the previous generation product, manufacturers in turn will be able to fairly accurately estimate the technological and manufacturing changes required to serve the customers' needs. In short, the

---

[11]Dorothy Leonard-Barton, Edith Wilson, and John Doyle, "Commercializing Technology: Imaginative Understanding of User Needs," Harvard Business School Working Paper #93-053.

customer's voice becomes the dominant impetus for new product design. Tools and techniques such as Quality Function Deployment (QFD) and Conjoint analysis are useful for such new product development activity.[12] Because customers know what they want, and because alternative solutions are usually available in the market, incremental innovations are often designed to meet narrow cost targets. Performance at a price, rather than performance alone becomes an important design criterion. Even if it did not apply to the whole product, certainly component parts could benefit from reverse engineering key competitors' products. The voice of the distribution channel has to be factored into the product launch. The product design and pricing has to be sensitive to channels' profit considerations. The key differences are captured in **Figure 4**.

Wrongly interpreted, **Figure 4** could misdirect managers into believing that minimal marketing input is required of breakthrough new products. Nothing could be farther from the truth. Even though only a few customers may be able to connect with the company's technology visions, it is important to remember that the success of the new product depends on the crucial element of the manufacturer being able to envision and build a market for its products. This often requires careful marketing thought up front. One has to identify potential markets and customers; a program to educate them on the benefits of the new technology must be mounted to coincide with the new product's launch. At times a radically new sales and distribution system may be necessary. All this means that even though only a few customers may lend their voice to technology development, the new product introduction process must recognize and incorporate the market building and development activity.

Figure 4   Nature of the Marketing Tasks

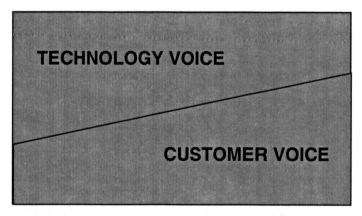

BREAKTHROUGH   INCREMENTAL
NEW PRODUCTS   NEW PRODUCTS

Marketing Tasks   Marketing Tasks

- Visioning the Market   - Listening to the market
- Building and creating   - Effectively and efficiently
  demand for the product   addressing existing demand

---

[12]Robert J. Dolan, "Managing the New Product Development Process," Addison-Wesley, Reading, Massachusetts, 1993.

In contrast, sales and manufacturing functions have a crucial role to play in developing and marketing incremental new products. That is because the sales/distribution channel is often the one that is closest to the customer and in the best position to read customer feedback. Many of the customer requirements may not necessitate fundamental technological innovation as much as feature and function improvements. The engineering/manufacturing discipline could many times be in a position to build these upgrades without resorting to an intense research/technology effort. Thus while R&D and Marketing may play the lead role in breakthrough new product development, usually Sales and Manufacturing/Engineering have a larger role to play in incremental new product development.

Mistake #1   The most common mistake is the utter lack of sensitivity to the differences in the management tasks required of incremental versus breakthrough projects. There is an overwhelming tendency to treat them all alike. It is important to realize that cross-functional involvement is not a panacea to all new product development problems; what matters is the nature of the cross-functional involvement (such as those shown in **Figure** 4). Time and again we found short-term-results-oriented line people assigned to breakthrough development teams. Not only were they unable to envision how the market would develop, their pessimistic forecasts dampened the teams' enthusiasm. They in turn were extremely frustrated because the teams were unable to meet their request for hard customer data or precise product cost estimates. The solution is not to leave the line functions (like Production and Sales) out, but instead to incorporate the right kind of Marketing and Manufacturing thinking into the team. But it certainly would be dangerous to leave it all to the inventors. Technical people who are thrilled with the "breakthrough" idea may be short sighted with respect to its commercial feasibilities. Their market forecasts may have a higher correlation to their aspirations for the product than to market realities. At the other extreme, incremental product teams may find themselves saddled with thinkers and visionaries who question the value of the new product concept, who often ask for a thorough systemwide evaluation of every product or process change. "What's so new about this new product?" they often ask. Yet the field-level sales people or the operations people on the team will vouch for its viability and urge a quick clearance to the next stage. They know the product will work and their customers will buy, if only the new product is brought speedily into the market. They are shocked by the project's snail's pace. The moral of the story is simple: Cross-functional teams require people of appropriate cross-functional abilities.

Mistake #2   Though not as common as #1, Mistake #2 is a tendency to assume that breakthrough projects equate with high profile activities needing resources and top management support, and that incremental projects are of less importance needing only a back-pocket support.

This is simply not true. The resource allocation decision has to be based on the long-term financial attractiveness of the project. Some breakthrough innovations may not have a large market potential to start with. The market will have to develop and grow with the adoption of the innovation. This being the case, it may be prudent to stage the allocation of resources on such projects. On the other hand, many incremental innovations may absolutely require a major investment up front. This is usually the case when the firm's existing product is hopelessly out-of-date in a very large market. Re-engineering the product may require heavy manufacturing investments. The point is simple: do not confuse the nature of the project with potential pay-offs. While it is almost inevitable that top management would have to get involved in high-investment projects, it is not entirely desirable to delegate all low-investment projects. Some of them may involve technologies or anticipated market niches that could be of great strategic importance to the company, and without top management's support in the early stages, such projects may flounder. Thus top management's involvement has to be selective and on a case-by-case basis, but certainly independent of the nature of the product.

In **Figure 3**, we referred to the north-south direction as the axis of mismatch. Here's where there's a divergence on the manufacturer's and customer's perception of the product's newness. In one case, the supplier of the technology may see the product as an incremental innovation, whereas the customer may perceive it as a breakthrough—we call this the Shadowed New Product (because the supplier may not see its true potential); and in the other case, the supplier may see the product as an incredible breakthrough, whereas the customers may be lukewarm toward it—we call this the Delusionary New Product. (See **Figure 5**.)

Shadowed New Products[13]

By "shadowed," we do not mean that the product's technical merit or the customer's potential benefit is negligible, but that the product's contribution in economic terms to the company's portfolio is relatively minor in the short run. These are products that the company's engineers and R&D scientists discovered while pursuing other more central projects. Alternatively, these are products that the company's sales force thought would serve some of the unmet needs of its existing customers. Either way, these products are not the central thrust of a company's R&D or sales strategy. These are products discovered in the shadow of other more important activity. Consequently, such products are not intended to account for a significant chunk of the company's revenues or profits. These are products like the Post-It note at 3M Company.

Figure 5   Seller-Customer Mismatch

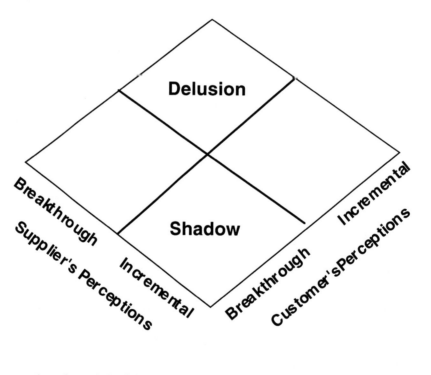

The story goes that the original Post-It application came out of division manager Arthur Fry's desire to keep the bookmark from falling out of his hymn book. There is a similar story regarding 3M's Scotch brand transparent tape. It was apparently invented for an industrial customer who used it to seal insulation in an airtight package. When first developed, both these products had limited application, and in fact the company was not even sure where the market was

---

[13]A large part of this discussion is drawn from V. Kasturi Rangan, Rajiv Lal and Ernie P. Maier, "Managing Marginal New Products," *Business Horizons*, Vol. 35, No. 5, pp.35-42.

for such products. The products were invented for a specific use, rather than to serve a whole market. But today Post-It and Scotch brand tape are in the top five office supply items in the United States, and represent a multimillion-dollar business for 3M company. When initially launched many such innovations appear marginal. All are small contributors individually, but down the road they could well turn out to have significant impact on a company's bottom line. However, very few companies pay attention to pro-actively marketing such products.

What reasons underlie the failed launches of so many such Shadow new products? The fundamental reason is that these products do not generate the same sense of urgency or focus that accompanies "central" new products. Even though the product idea may have clear champions, because the product was invented relatively cheaply, the new product development team usually will not subject it to the same taxing commercial feasibility and test-marketing standards as the other central products in its pipeline. Many times such products bypass established processes to fall right into the hands of day-to-day line management. Commercialization usually follows organizational routines. And therein lies the crux of the problem.

Mistake #3   Because managers already handle a portfolio of other products through existing manufacturing-sales systems, it makes sense to adopt the same for the new product. But the true appreciation for the new product in many cases comes from new customers in new segments, and even if they come from current customers, a different buying unit with different buying criteria may be responsible for its adoption. Using existing organizational systems often means completely missing the boat on the real customer and his real needs. This is the customer who values the products as a breakthrough.

A frequent practice is to "make a little, sell a little," until the opportunity is crystal clear. Since the product is not central to the company's short-term financial well being, there is a tendency to look for some signs of success toward which further attention and resources may be directed. Taking advantage of the existing organizational routines is certainly the cost-minimizing approach; sharing product management, sales management, and distribution is one outcome. Using common marketing and sales resources makes the most economic sense at the outset, with the intention of ultimately tailoring a program for the new product. But the product must show some initial signs of success, so managers "wait and see." Meanwhile a huge opportunity is being missed. It is sold as an incremental innovation to existing customers, when with a little imagination and creativity, an entirely new problem for an entirely new customer may be addressed. Market segmentation and channel selection is usually wrong, and because the product is anchored to existing solutions, it is usually under-priced. A higher price can be obtained, but that requires active customer education for the right customers.

Marketing is as much about creating and shaping customer needs as it is about serving well-identified customer requirements. Good marketers learn about and shape customer needs, even as they implement their marketing programs. The "business as usual" approach completely violates the interactive nature of this market development process.

While the "wait-and-see" and "business-as-usual" attitudes may be interpreted as a failing of management execution, top management must take its share of the blame, too. It is responsible for providing a corporate environment/culture that encourages entrepreneurship with rewards for success that outweigh the risks of failure. With a "strategic" new product, top management involvement is easily obtained. Decisions involving development, introduction, marketing and sales occur at the top level. This allows senior management to make far-reaching choices and motivate the organization to reflect its priorities. In the case of shadowed new products, the decision to launch has neither strategic urgency nor the routine expediency of a product enhancement. Under these circumstances, lower-level management has no incentive to take initiative either, because success may not get the attention of the top brass, whereas a failure will only unnecessarily diminish an existing reputation. The end result is a vicious cycle of "wait-and-see" and "business-as-usual," which accelerates the death of the product, followed by a quiet burial. This is a pity because these products cost very little to invent and make, but with imaginative marketing they could add significant new customer segments and new products for the company. Each new product by itself may not immediately be a significant contribution to the bottom line, but put together they certainly bring a substantial muscle to the company.

Delusionary New Products

We take up these products last because they represent the largest proportion of new product failures. These are innovations where the suppliers of the technology have grandiose visions for the product, but their customers often do not share the same euphoria. We outlined the predicament of NeXT early in the article, but there are literally hundreds more examples like that.[14] Barabba and Zaltman describe the VideoDisc fiasco[15]:

> Another example of how technology cannot stand on its own, no matter how advanced, is provided by RCA's $580 million VideoDisc venture. R&D made a major technological breakthrough that had many technological merits, such as a higher-quality (relative to VCR technology) means for watching movies at home; yet, because of improper analysis of the desires of the market, the venture failed. . .

> . . . RCA's VideoDisc strategy had been heavily dependent on a few key assumptions: that the traditional mass-market customer would prefer a low price to more features, that dealers could clear up any consumer confusion about multiple formats, that VCR producers could not substantially reduce the price gap between their players and disc players, that dealers would welcome disc systems as they had VCRs, and that consumers would want to own video programming just as they owned LP records and audio tapes. . .

> . . . In fact, the outcome quickly revealed that most of the key assumptions on which RCA had based its VideoDisc strategy were no longer valid...Had the plan been for a stable product in a familiar business, it would have been well-conceived and well-executed, but for an innovative product in a marketplace destabilized by changing technologies, it was an approach that allowed little room for adjustment.

Why are there so many products with more Show than Tell? Don't these firms understand the discipline of knowing the customer? Don't they collect market research? Many do, but the disconnect, unfortunately, comes because of an "inside-out" process rather than a lack of customer information. As a result, the data interpretation is faulty, not necessarily the data collection. Because of the newness of the product, the technology, or the manufacturing process to the company, there's a justifiable air of expectation and excitement within. Whether potential customers are equally as excited is the real question. To them, this product may just be an additional line for consideration among the various available alternatives. They would perhaps like to know why the said offering is superior to competitive products. In their minds, they are viewing an incremental innovation rather than a breakthrough invention.

---

[14]Donald W. Hendon, *Classic Failures in Product Marketing*, Quorum Books, New York, 1989.
[15]:Vincent P. Barabba and Gerald Zaltman, *Hearing the Voice of the Market*, Harvard Business School Press, 1991, pp. 31-32.

Mistake #4   Such supplier misperceptions lead to faulty product positioning. There is an attempt to break new ground with the product, when in fact a "new and improved" positioning would be more palatable to the customer. The Sony Walkman product launch process is a nice illustration of how to do it right.[16] The product development effort required tricky coordination between its Tape Recorder and Headphone divisions. The whole idea of making a cassette player without a speaker or a recorder, but instead with a headphone, seemed quite at odds with Sony's product traditions. The concept itself would not have been commercially viable without the amazing speed of its product development team. The scale-up required innovative manufacturing techniques. Yet when the product was launched, it was priced at a modest $165, with a clear goal to bring it down to less than $100 within 3 years. The product was sold through broad line electronic distribution channels. In short, the product was positioned, priced and sold as though it was an additional offering in the mass-distributed, modestly priced consumer electronic category of tape recorders, radios, and cameras.

Of course, we are not suggesting that all potential delusionary products be priced and marketed through mass-market channels. Our argument is that they should be positioned and priced appropriately with respect to existing solutions in the marketplace. If such an effort in fact requires the company to go upmarket for a specific customer niche where the product outperforms existing solutions, by all means it should be marketed and channeled to reflect its premium status. Our point is that the positioning strategy be driven by the market, rather than by the ambitions of the product champions. The outcome of such as exercise could in some cases lead to the conclusion that there are no equivalent customer solutions in the market and that, in fact, the product is a radical new idea. The inventors then have a clear breakthrough on their hands, and marketing resources would be needed to develop and create a market.

Conclusions

The mismatches, that is the Shadows and Delusions, could be corrected by aligning them to Breakthroughs or Incrementals. But it is important to drive the analysis at all times, from the customers' viewpoint. A proper alignment will not automatically lead to new product success. It requires a careful piloting through the 13 steps indicated in **Figure 1**. The nature of the new product development process and the composition of the teams and the nature of their tasks will have to carefully reflect the nature of the new product. All this is hard work and creative work. But at least if the ideas are right, and when accompanied by good execution, the chances of success are maximized. On the other hand, if the alignment is mismatched no amount of creativity and executional excellence can remedy a guaranteed failure.

---

[16]P. Ranaganath Nayak & John M. Ketteringham, *Breakthroughs*, Mercury, 1993, pp. 94-111.

Exhibit 1   New Product Taxonomies

1. Ansoff H. Igor (1957), "Market Strategy Given Newness of Markets and Products," *Harvard Business Review,* September-October.

	Existing Products	New Products
New Markets	Market Development	Diversification
Existing Markets	Market Penetration	Product Development

2. Booz, Allen and Hamilton (1982), *New Products Management for the 1980s,* New York: Booz, Allen and Hamilton.

NEWNESS TO MARKET

	LOW		HIGH
HIGH		New Product Lines (20%)	New-to-World Products (10%)
NEWNESS TO COMPANY	Improvements/ Revisions to Existing Products (26%)	Additions to Existing Product Lines (26%)	
LOW	Cost Reductions (11%)	Repositionings (7%)	

Exhibit 1 (continued)

3. Steven C. Wheelwright and Kim B. Clark (1992), "Creating Project Plans to Focus Product Development," *Harvard Business Review*, March-April.

PROCESS CHANGES

PRODUCT CHANGES	New Core Process	Next Generation	Upgrade	Tuning/ Incremental

New Core Product	**Break-through**	
Next Generation Product		Platform
Addition to Product Family		
Add-ons and Enhancements		Derivative

DEFINING NEXT-GENERATION PRODUCTS: AN INSIDE LOOK

(B. Tabrizi and R. Walleigh / #97610 / 9 p)

Summary

The authors completed a study of 28 next-generation product-development projects in 14 leading high-tech companies. They found that most of the companies were unable to complete projects on schedule and also had difficulty creating the the derivative products needed to fill the market gaps that their next-generation products would create. The problem in every case was rooted in the product-definition phase. Not coincidentally, the successful companies in the study had all learned how to handle the technical and marketplace uncertainties in their product-definition processes. The authors have developed a set of best practices that can measurably improve the product-definition phase at any company.

Outline

Product Strategy
Project Organization
Execution During Definition
Beyond New-Platform Development

Learning Objectives

- Become acquainted with the principles and techniques that optimize the earliest stages of next-generation product development
- Understand the common pitfalls that sabotage early product development

Questions, Ideas, and Exercises

1. An important principle that successful companies understand is the need to bring depth and substance to certain key activities even at the earliest, and presumably the fuzziest, stages of product development. One example is the product mapping process: in successful companies, all relevant senior managers built their maps as a team, within a larger organizational context that fostered communication. These managers also understood that the maps were dynamic, needing to be changed and revisited often; as a result, their maps were powerful planning tools, continually becoming more useful, rather than mere sketches. Another example of the "get deep fast" principle is prototyping: Successful firms plunged quickly into the creation of rough prototypes, revealing fundamental strengths and flaws before vast resources were committed. (You will see this idea echoed in the case study on IDEO included in this book.) How well do the product-development processes at your company follow this principle?

2. Consider the diagram that illustrates "cyclical workload mismatch." The authors identify a need to manage workflow as burdens on the various functional teams ease or intensify. Has this mismatch occurred at your company? Are the builders of products ("engineers," in the authors' example) too burdened to work on derivatives and enhancements when the optimal time comes? Are the marketers similarly strapped when the new-platform launch is being finished? Might a scheduled break help to ease this problem? Note the authors' observation that companies that took such a break in new-product development "lost no momentum between launch…and execution."

3. Successful companies use documents shrewdly and effectively. One example is the product-priority document, which reorganizes the standard product-requirements document into categories from the customer's point of view -- "must have," "should have," and "nice to have." Is your company using its basic documents to maximum effect? Consider the documents that capture your product plans. Are they designed to link product development to the company's overall business strategy? Are they configured to reveal the perspective of customers, suppliers, and other key stakeholders? Or are they "hollow" documents that fail to give the product-development team a sense of urgency and a clear picture of design tradeoffs?

Defining Next-Generation Products: An Inside Look

by Behnam Tabrizi and Rick Walleigh

Harvard Business Review

Reprint 97610

Defining Next-Generation

How leading high-tech companies successfully develop new products.

THE CREATION of next-generation products and their derivatives would seem to be the routine work of technology-based companies. Their continued business success, after all, depends on it.

Yet in a detailed study of 28 next-generation product-development projects at 14 leading high-tech companies, we found that most of the companies were unable to complete such projects on schedule. Furthermore, they had difficulty developing the derivative products needed to fill the gaps in the market that their next-generation products would create. Of the companies we studied – which ranged in size from $500 million to more than $10 billion in annual sales – the next-generation products of only four successfully met their developers' expectations about schedule, specification, and market share. The next-generation products of five companies appeared successful to outside observers but did not meet internal goals or market-share aspirations. The new products of the remaining five companies were wholly unsuccessful. We also found that in every case where delays and difficulties occurred, they originated in the definition phase of the company's product-development process – that is, before the organization had committed itself to a specific product design.

Next-generation products – also known as platform products because they are expected to inspire and support a whole new line of derivative products – require a major commitment of resources. Like Volvo's 850, which introduced five-cylinder, front-wheel-drive cars to the company's line, and Boeing's 777, which substantially improved on the range and efficiency of its 737 line of aircraft, a platform product incorporates significant improvements in performance and cost over the preceding

Products: An Inside Look

by Behnam Tabrizi and
Rick Walleigh

generation's product. It addresses the needs of future customers while providing a path for current customers to migrate from the older product.[1]

A panel of consulting and academic experts picked the 14 companies that we examined. Guarantees of anonymity helped ensure our access to the companies' most sensitive internal information and to candid interviews with people at every level. We had access, for instance, to business and product-definition plans, team meeting minutes, information about product development processes, and postproject assessments.

What sets the adept minority of these companies apart from the rest? The nine companies that failed to meet their own expectations did so for many different reasons, but the successful companies were all successful for the same reasons. Thus we have been able to discern from the latter group's actions

a set of best practices that can measurably improve the definition phase – or "fuzzy front end" – of any company's product-development process.

We have not discovered a magic formula for rapid, successful new-product definition. Because new-platform products are developed to serve the future needs of customers, companies are at high risk when they work with new, unproved technologies or architectures. Furthermore, given the volatile nature of their industries, high-tech companies have difficulty predicting how their markets will move over time. Uncertainty promotes bickering among groups within the organization and indecision by managers – and leads to chaos in product development.

The successful companies we studied had all learned to deal with the technical and marketplace uncertainties. That is, they had learned how to

overcome the chaos in their product definition processes. And while they all used roughly the same techniques, they had derived those techniques quite independently. We have grouped the techniques into three categories: *product strategy, project organization,* and *execution during the*

It is in the nature of platform products to expose greater markets than they can cover.

definition stage.[2] These categories do not encompass everything a company needs to do as it defines a platform product. Rather, they provide a useful way to cluster and think about the best practices we have identified.

Product Strategy

We have bunched three best practices for product development under the rubric of product strategy. The first is to create a clear map of the company's product stream for the next two years and to use it to manage all aspects of the company's development activities. The second is to generate a seamless product strategy – that is, one that leaves no holes for competitors to exploit. The third is to collect, interpret, and assimilate good information about the market.

Creating and Using a Map of the Company's New-Product Stream. Most companies use some sort of strategic-planning process to clarify their vision and then map the product development activity required to realize it. The maps define a stream of products, including platform products and their derivatives, that the company is committed to developing over the next two years. The main value of the maps lies not in any certainty about the future that they might imply. Indeed, the maps are revised frequently. Rather, they help force the company to make decisions about new projects for platform products amid the uncertainty that characterizes rapidly shifting markets and evolving technologies.

All the companies in our study had product maps. The differences between the successes and the failures lay in how they used the maps as management tools.

The organizational process used to build commitment among senior managers while they create a product map is critical. One successful company draws its product maps at senior management re-

treats in order to promote cohesion, commitment, and clarity throughout the organization regarding the sequence and timing of new products. In that setting, all managers, regardless of their function, begin to grasp the significance of the new products for the organization – how and when they will have an impact on marketing, distribution, technology, and service. Mapping also illuminates major resource decisions affecting the execution of the new-platform product. The process of creating a map forces senior management to face up to tough choices – whether to increase funding for a product line in order to become a market leader, when and where to dampen support for maturing products, and how to tackle the inevitable trade-offs between promising individual projects and overall strategic direction.

Once drawn, maps are not set in concrete. The volatility of technology and technology markets permits no such luxury. The company referred to above holds its senior management retreats every six months and redraws the map at each retreat. Furthermore, the senior management team revisits and updates its plans bimonthly between retreats so that the document is always current.

In the underperforming companies we studied, the product maps were two-dimensional charts lacking in substance. They gave senior managers the false sense that future plans were in place. In fact, however, little if any thought had been given to budgets, organizational issues, or technology requirements. Consequently, the maps had no value as planning tools, and every step of the product definition process generated its own crisis.

The senior members of one troubled platform-project team we examined spent two years revising their definition of the product while marketing and manufacturing maintained their own separate definitions. When asked later about their overarching strategy for the product, the senior members claimed that they had been too busy to address such broad issues earlier. The company's mapping process was a hollow exercise that did not force anyone to anticipate such questions. Not surprisingly, the entire organization remained confused

Behnam Tabrizi is a consulting professor in the Department of Industrial Engineering and Engineering Management at Stanford University in Stanford, California. He consults with leading high-tech companies on product development and market acceptance. Rick Walleigh is a partner at Ernst & Young in San Jose, California; he also consults with leading high-tech companies.

about the product and its market positioning right up to the time of its introduction.

In contrast, another company we examined demonstrated the value of the mapping process when it had to choose among 50 proposed projects. It used its map to define key priorities, reach timely decisions, and define the new-platform products. Furthermore, because of the efficiency introduced by the mapping process, the company could downsize its development organization and use the savings to fund several marketing initiatives and a strategically critical acquisition. Thus the process of mapping not only yields better results in final products but also eliminates wasted effort that distracts an organization from more important work. In the best companies, the product maps and the processes used to create them are the centerpiece of the entire product-development process.

Building a Product Strategy Without Holes. It is in the nature of platform products to expose greater markets than they themselves cover. Successful companies make plans to fill those holes with derivative products even while they are defining the platform product that will create the gaps. Companies that don't make such plans hand rich opportunities to their competitors, who may even dislodge them from the very markets that they have created. (See the exhibit "Platform Products and the Gaps They Create.")

The successful companies we studied made sure they understood who was buying their current products and why, so that they could make informed judgments about the gaps in the market that their new products would create. Then they could decide how to protect those gaps – and their existing markets – from new entrants. Several companies made their existing offerings more attractive by discounting, adding new features, or running promotional pricing campaigns. They also quickly offered scaled-down versions of their new products in order to hold on to the low end of the market they had just created. (See the insert "Dreams and Nightmares.")

Getting Good Market Information. Effective product definition demands good market information. The companies we found to be successful at introducing new-platform products maintained continual, open-ended conversations with their customers. In particular, those companies made an effort to identify the pioneers and risk takers among their customers – the people most likely to push the existing products to their performance limits. Product team leaders maintained an ongoing dialogue with those leading-edge customers, sharing information about technical trends, predictions made in

Platform Products and the Gaps They Create

New-platform products create marketplace gaps that competitors can exploit. Companies should plan to fill the gaps with derivative products even while they are defining the new platform itself.

the trade press, and updates on progress and possible applications of new products. Team leaders asked pointed questions: What would help your company accomplish its objectives? What new features would be useful? What are your cost constraints? What features could be eliminated to meet your needs at the right cost?

But successful companies talked to more than just current customers. They developed processes to query prospective customers, indirect sales channels such as retailers and wholesalers, clients of current customers, and even former customers. Those companies were determined to develop assessments of the potential success of new products that would be untainted by the bias of their largest and most supportive customers. They wanted to know, in other words, what the market expected.

Project Organization

The organizational characteristics of a company's platform-product-development process are crucial to its timely and effective execution. Our study uncovered three best practices relating to project organization. The first is the willingness to turn the development of new-platform products over to business units created solely for that purpose. The second is knowing how to choose the optimum number of members – with the right mix of skills – for the product definition team over the course of the product development process. And the third is the ability to match other product-development resources – such as the shifting workloads of engineers and marketers – to the cyclical demands of the process.

Creating New Business Units for New Markets. When a company intends its new-platform product to make a quantum leap in performance in comparison with the current product, it will probably need to design a completely new product system and architecture. Moreover, the new product is likely to be addressed more to new customers than to users of the current product. With that in mind, the successful companies in our study sometimes created new business units to develop the new-platform product. They found that internal cultures and processes honed to support one kind of product were ill-suited to the creation and support of a significantly different one. Managers told us that in such situations product development would fare better in a newly created division.

One company, for instance, assigned seasoned talent from three separate product groups to a new division with the sole objective of creating a new family of products. Another corporation used the facilities of a recently acquired company to house a new project team thousands of miles (and several time zones) away from corporate headquarters. The team itself consisted largely of new hires people with strong engineering backgrounds, a desire for visible results, and little patience for bureaucratic procedures.

In both cases, the companies encouraged the newly formed groups to behave entrepreneurially; that is, to create their own three-year business plans and to begin generating revenue as quickly as possible by cobbling together products that would get them into the market – all the while working on the new-platform design. Both companies supported the new units through the loan of corporate resources from marketing, distribution, and sales – resources that would help the new enterprise gain an early foothold in the market it was targeting.

Staffing the Platform-Product-Definition Team. Assigning too many people to platform-product-definition teams too early can delay the definition process and blunt the results. One company assigned more than 30 engineers to the formative phase of a development project, causing a senior manager to complain that "we had too many engineers spinning their wheels while the definition kept changing." Now the company begins new projects with no more than five engineers and one market strategist to define the overall framework. It adds new people to work on the details after the small team has fixed the initial specifications.

Dreams and Nightmares

Intel Corporation is a master at filling in the holes it creates by introducing new-platform products. It introduced the Pentium microprocessor to the personal computer market at 60 and 66 MHz clock speeds in March 1993; over time, it released successively faster versions that recently reached beyond 200 MHz. Each release involved a price cut that was made possible by cost reductions. The company also brought out compact versions of the chip for the laptop and notebook markets. Thus Intel quickly filled all the performance, price, and application gaps caused by the Pentium and so preempted the competition – every marketer's dream. Similarly, when the company introduced its new-platform Pentium Pro microprocessor, it rapidly filled the market niches created by that chip. In addition, the new microprocessor worked with software applications designed for previous Pentium chips, thus providing a migration path to the new product for existing customers. And in 1997, the company plugged the gap in the multimedia market by introducing what it called *MMX technology*. The technology allowed the company's microprocessors, including the Pentium, to operate effectively with audio, video, games, and graphics.

Orion Computer (a composite fiction), on the other hand, experienced a nightmare. Orion, a worldwide leader in engineering workstations, introduced a feature-laden model for the networked-engineering-design market seven months behind schedule. The result of a year's intensive, often chaotic planning followed by two years' design and development, the next-generation product boasted an advanced central-processing unit, exclusive graphics capability, and even flexible internal-networking circuitry. But the chaotic development process not only had created costly delays but also had depressed morale on the development team to the point that several key employees left the company. Then, after a couple of months of successful sales, Orion saw its new market undermined by a competitor's product that offered fewer features and functions than its own but at a much lower price. Orion had nothing to counter the newcomer with and thus surrendered sales and share in the market that its own platform product had created.

In addition to needing the right number of employees, an effective platform-product-definition team requires people with the right mix of skills and experience. Senior marketing strategists with a grasp of technology and a feel for the direction of markets and key competitors are best equipped to define new opportunities. Their senior technical counterparts can articulate the possible technological obstacles, cost and time constraints, and risks. Their seniority and experience gives both functional types the credibility and authority needed to make decisions that cannot easily be overturned and muffles costly second-guessing by others on the team or in management.

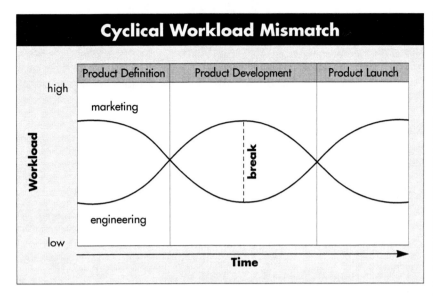

Cyclical Workload Mismatch

The extensive experience these senior marketing and technical staff have acquired should give them a broader perspective than others on the team. Thus they should emerge as influential leaders during all stages of the product development process, tempering the tendency of less-experienced engineers to tweak and fiddle with a design long after it should have been set and discouraging marketers from summarily discounting technical hurdles in a rush to get the product out.

We found that product definition was most successful when initial specifications preceded the final selection of the product development team. We also found that products emerged faster and made more of an impact on the market when product teams included the company's most knowledgeable engineers and marketing strategists from the outset. And we noted that when product development teams were thus staffed, a company's ability to follow through with derivative products, follow-on applications, and ongoing product enhancements was also much greater.

Matching Resources During New-Platform Development. All 14 companies we studied used cross-functional product-development teams, but the successful companies effectively addressed a problem inherent in using such teams. We call the problem *cycle mismatch*. Early in the product development process – in the product definition stage – a team's marketing professionals are busy writing preliminary business plans and, with input from the engineers, determining the market's requirements. The engineers have a lighter load at this stage, but their workload increases as the product's architecture and specifications are developed.

Then, during the product development stage, the bulk of the work falls on the engineers. The marketers are much less busy – their role is to watch customers and competitors for shifts in the marketplace. Later, during the product launch stage, the burden on the engineers begins to ease while the work of the marketing people grows as they prepare to promote, deliver, and support the new product. (See the exhibit "Cyclical Workload Mismatch.")

As the relative burden on engineers and marketing professionals reverses, the company may lose the opportunity to begin work on derivative products and new-product enhancements. Such missed opportunities happen because engineers must wait for the now busy marketing managers to finish the new-platform launch before those managers can help define other new products.

To correct this imbalance, the successful project teams we studied took a scheduled break – which was shown on the companies' product-stream maps – midway through development of the new-platform product. During this brief pause, the team – marketing professionals included – sought to identify markets that would be affected by the new product, to initiate the development of derivatives to fill potentially vulnerable areas, and to assign key engineering and marketing people to the development task.

The companies that took this approach lost no momentum between the launch of their new-platform products and the execution of a seamless market-penetration strategy. As marketers became preoccupied in the later stages of product development, engineers already had the specifications they needed to continue the technical progress on derivative products – and on adding to or enhancing the new-platform product's features. The successful companies all used this approach to create entire families of products by filling the gaps around the new platforms. Thus they created barriers to encroachment on their expanded markets.

Scheduling a pause part way into the product development process does not by itself ensure the development and introduction of derivative and enhanced products. To fully correct the cycle mismatch during the definition of new-platform products, companies need to be sure that four other elements are also in place:

- discipline, which requires the company to establish explicit milestones for a derivative-product-development plan when it is mapping its product stream;
- incentives that reward the members of the marketing and engineering team for success in filling gaps in the marketplace, not just in meeting new-product requirements;
- alignment, which means that senior managers' incentives must be tied to their effectiveness in directing attention to planning for derivative products during the development process; and
- resources ensuring the availability of sufficient key members of the product development team to work on derivative products and platform product enhancements.

The companies successful at filling the gaps around new platforms tended to release new or upgraded products frequently. This rapid-fire approach to product releases forced those organizations to stay abreast of new technology and to look at product development as a continual process. The frequent release of products also helped those companies appeal to many market segments with customized offerings. Necessarily, the companies considered the issues of modularity and scale when they developed a platform product so that they could develop and release derivatives quickly.

Execution During Definition

By *execution during definition*, we refer not to how the best-practice companies actually defined their new-platform products, but to how they tried to ensure that the definition process took place effectively and on schedule. We include three best practices under this third and final rubric.

Tracking Progress and Sustaining Urgency. The root causes of most of the delays we observed during product definition were managerial in nature: the lack of a process to monitor elapsed time and insufficient management attention to the routine aspects of the definition process. Only a few of the 14 organizations maintained a disciplined process for measuring adherence to schedule and the effectiveness of the definition in the earliest stages of a new-platform project. More often, until very late in the product development process, only crises got

The successful companies released products frequently to fill gaps around new platforms.

management's attention. As a result, product launches were late, unfocused, and unsupported by contingency plans or additional resources.

One of the successful companies, however, starts an internal clock as soon as the first meeting about the new-platform product takes place. Thereafter, the company tracks not just time elapsed but also the cost in time of the personnel involved. Doing so establishes and helps maintain a sense of urgency among product-development team members.

Another tool used by managers in the successful companies is a so-called product-priority document. This is nothing more than the traditional product-requirements document, but with required features organized into categories from the customer's point of view. The three categories are "must have," "should have," and "nice to have." Creating the product-priority document forces teams to analyze various trade-offs in detailed discussions with customers. "If we add this feature," the team will ask a customer, "our cost will grow by x dollars and our development schedule will be slowed by y months. Are you willing to pay more and wait longer?"

The product-priority document links the product introduction to the company's overall business strategy and keeps product developers focused on the features that customers want in the order in which they want them. It holds the team to firm deadlines and clear agreements about trade-offs. This approach encourages but at the same time disciplines the "what if" discussions that can delay new-platform development.

The product-priority document intensifies the focus on the new product across functional and managerial lines. And it sets the pace for the product's introduction by establishing a priority of features. If competitive conditions change and it becomes important to enter the market sooner than originally planned, the important but lower-priority features can be held for inclusion in the next set of products.

The best-practice companies employ a third technique to sustain urgency. Senior members of the product team – both engineers and marketers – meet early in the process with senior management and decide how long the team will be allowed to "play in the sand" – that is, how much time it will have to create a definition of the new product. And senior managers continue to meet weekly with these senior team members to check their progress against the schedule and to review the team's resource needs.

In one company, after a new-platform definition and milestones had emerged, the project entered what the company called the *commitment gate* – a mechanism for freezing the platform definition and specifications. At that point, team members and senior managers articulated and understood all requirements. The development team committed to a delivery date, and everyone involved knew that only dramatic changes in technology, markets, or corporate resources could reopen those decisions.

The companies that used a commitment-gate model continued to gather information from customers and others right through the product launch. They did not ignore the market as it changed around them, but they were in a position to know which changes could wait to be accommodated later, with derivative products. Most companies in our study lacked a commitment gate. Various parts of the organizations were continually changing product definitions, in some cases until just weeks before the launch date – thus inducing delay after delay.

Developing Early Prototypes. The successful companies we studied moved quickly to develop prototypes of the key subsystems of their new prod-

Early prototypes excited and energized the product team in ways that less palpable representations of the new product or its subsystems could not. With prototypes available, team members' discussions were more focused and concrete, and decisions were made more quickly.

Successful organizations also found that customers are willing editors and critics. When given a working model or system component for comment, they talked about the features they liked, desirable attributes they missed, and a variety of interface and ergonomic issues (screens and switches, for example). The feedback provided by customers at this stage helped product developers reconcile desired features with the constraints of time and cost.

Successful companies also stayed in touch with customers, even as late as the week the new products were shipped, to gather information about potential needs and early changes that could be incorporated into future versions of the product. Those companies have created processes that allow them to maintain close relationships with their customers throughout the product's introduction and its refinement. The customer dialogue doesn't delay product development. Rather, it provides a continuous stream of market information that helps shape derivatives and revisions.

Using Development Partnerships. A few of the companies we studied elected to form partnerships with key suppliers to develop new-platform products. In some cases, the codeveloper brought a set of skills and experiences that complemented the strengths of the marketing partner; in others, the partner offered financial resources or useful technology. In several cases, however, major differences in style, priorities, and motivation created costly delays and revisions.

Most of the issues that threatened to derail the codevelopment ventures were resolved at the working level, not by contract amendments or litigation. Project leaders found that when companies shared people and technology, the differences narrowed and momentum was regained. That was particularly true when cooperating companies shared engineers – by swapping them between companies, for instance, or by having engineers from both companies work together at a single site. Any issues in one organization – specifications, standards, or milestones, for instance – quickly became matters of common concern.

Engineers working closely together on site developed a common language and a common set of tools

Product team members met early with senior management to decide how long the team would be allowed to "play in the sand."

uct – and then of the entire system. Because they skipped the usual proof-of-concept stage, their prototypes often weren't perfect, requiring software fixes, rewiring, and even minor redesign. But the delays thus incurred were small and cheap relative to the advantages gained.

New-Product-Definition Processes

	Platform products	Derivative products
Uncertainty	High	Low
Definition of specifications	Specifications evolve over time before final definition	Specifications are completed within a few days
Initial staffing of team	Staffed with only key employees	Fully staffed with all employees involved in product development
Milestones	Early: Long intervals between milestones Later: Short intervals	Short intervals between well-defined milestones

and methodologies to use in developing the new product. One successful codeveloper reported that exchanges of engineers allowed each company to monitor the progress of the entire project with greater certainty. Using a common methodology, engineers from both companies were able to check the alignment of their individual efforts frequently and spot potential problems early. Their growing comfort with the codevelopment process enabled both partners to proceed confidently with their respective portions of the project. Like allied armies, codeveloping partners can surmount differences in style and culture when they are working together in pursuit of shared goals.

Beyond New-Platform Development

When a company treats the successful launch of a new-platform product as an isolated event rather than part of an ongoing process, competitors with imitative products can quickly take possession of the market gap the new platform creates. The companies we studied reported concern and frustration as they watched other companies exploit opportunities they had overlooked. So it is important to note once again that overall market success depends not only on a company's development of new-platform products but also on its ability to create the derivative products that can insulate its share of the market from competitors' incursions. The process entailed in defining derivative products, however, is markedly different from the process for defining platform products.

While the uncertainty surrounding new-platform-product definition requires a small, focused

working group, a derivatives team needs to be fully staffed at the outset to develop a comprehensive plan for reaching the target markets rapidly. And good process management necessitates the short-term tracking of goals for derivatives teams, with an emphasis on measuring their progress toward key milestones. (See the chart "New-Product-Definition Processes.")

Among the successful companies we studied, the effective derivatives teams launched their work with an off-site meeting to reach consensus on the requirements, detailed supporting plans, and timetable. Scheduling was especially critical, and key milestones were set at short intervals for easy monitoring. Action plans contained crisp, clear goals, and as the process proceeded, teams recognized individual members for meeting interim milestones and thus keeping the project on track.

A communications-networking company in our study deployed a separate team for derivative development while the new-platform-product project was still under way. The two-track process enabled the platform-product-definition team to distinguish genuine technical obstacles in its path (the "showstoppers") from difficulties the derivatives team could address in periodic upgrades (the "fixies"). This ability allowed the platform development team to retain its urgency.

As postreengineered companies look for ways to grow their businesses after a long campaign to reduce their costs, the best practices of successful product developers can help them capture new markets without major delays. Instead of leaving gaps for competitors to exploit, the successful companies we examined have learned how to define and develop new products in order to maximize their market penetration. Their lessons can be instructive for any manager facing the uncertainty that goes with developing products for a fast-paced global marketplace.

1. The definition of platform product is taken from Kim B. Clark and Steven C. Wheelwright, *Managing New Product and Process Development* (New York: The Free Press, 1993).

2. The authors thank Steven C. Wheelwright, M.B.A. Class of 1949 Professor of Business Administration at the Harvard Business School, for suggesting these three categories.

Reprint 97610

To place an order, call 800-988-0886.

DEVELOPING PRODUCTS ON INTERNET TIME

(M. Iansiti and A. MacCormack / #97505 / 10 p)

Summary

In today's world the market needs that a product is meant to satisfy and the technologies required to satisfy them can change radically, even as the product is under development. In response to such factors, companies in turbulent environments have had to modify the traditional product-development process, in which design implementation begins only once a product's concept has been determined in its entirety. Such companies have pioneered a flexible process that allows designers to define and shape products even after implementation has begun.

Outline

A Flexible Process at Work
The Foundations of a Flexible Process
  Sensing the Market
  Testing Technical Solutions
  Integrating Customer Needs with Technical Solutions
Putting Flexibility to the Test

Learning Objectives

- Understand the key features of a flexible product-design process
- Explore the uses of customer input and technical information and the integration of these two in final design

Questions, Ideas, and Exercises

1. Early in their article the authors distinguish between business environments that are predictable or evolving slowly and environments that are "turbulent." Is there internal consensus at your company about which type of environment you operate in? Try polling some of your colleagues on this point. If the consensus is that your environment is turbulent, consider the steps you are taking to build greater flexibility into product development. For example, have your product-development processes changed during the past twelve months to "delay until as late as possible any commitment to a final design configuration"? Are you continuously monitoring surveying customers and monitoring competitors? When you've acquired information from these sources, do your systems enable you to immediately integrate the acquired knowledge with your technical resources?

2. In the section entitled "Sensing the Market," consider the examples of Yahoo! and Fiat. These companies used their Web sites to do concept and product testing with customers. Might this approach work for your latest product-development efforts?

You might be surprised at how eager many customers are to give input on product-development questionnaires. And, as the authors point out in the example of Fiat, using your Web site can dramatically reduce the cost of a customer survey. But note, too, that Fiat gathered information in this way only from customers who came to the Fiat Web site and clicked on the link to the survey -- a limited subset of the prospective market for Fiat's new model.

Developing Products
on Internet Time

by Marco Iansiti and Alan MacCormack

Harvard Business Review

Reprint 97505

In today's turbulent business environments, more and more companies need a development process that embraces change – not one that resists it.

DEVELOPING PRODUCTS

by Marco Iansiti and Alan MacCormack

The rise of the World Wide Web has provided one of the most challenging environments for product development in recent history. The market needs that a product is meant to satisfy and the technologies required to satisfy them can change radically – even as the product is under development. In response to such factors, companies have had to modify the traditional product-development process in which design implementation begins only once a product's concept has been determined in its entirety. Instead, they have pioneered a *flexible* product-development process that allows designers to continue to define and shape products even after implementation has begun. This innovation enables Internet companies to incorporate rapidly changing customer requirements and evolving technologies into their designs until the last possible moment before a product is introduced to the market.

Flexible product development has been most fully realized in the Internet environment because of the turbulence found there, but the foundations for it exist in a wide range of industries where the need for responsiveness is paramount. Product developers in industries from computer workstations to banking increasingly face dynamic and unpredictable environments characterized by rapidly evolving technologies, changing customer tastes, and sweeping regulatory changes. In these industries, companies that have begun to adopt more flexible product-development approaches are setting new competitive standards.

What's involved in increasing the flexibility of the product development process? Many of the companies we studied have adopted a coherent set of mechanisms that allow product developers to generate and respond to new information about

 PHOTOS: LEFT, GERALD FRENCH/FPG; RIGHT, MIKE WILSON/FPG

ON INTERNET TIME

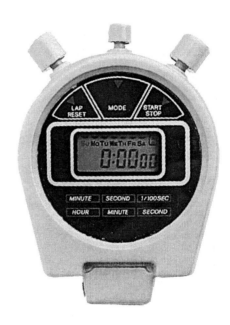

what customers want and about how technology has evolved over the course of a project. These mechanisms not only enable a continuous flow of information about customer needs and new technologies but also reduce both the cost and the time it takes to integrate that information into the evolving product design. They allow designers continually *to sense* customer needs, *to test* alternative technical solutions, and *to integrate* the acquired knowledge into a coherent product design. This flexible process continues iteratively throughout the development process.

The traditional development processes that many companies use are highly structured. A future product is designed, developed, transferred to production, and rolled out to the market in clearly articulated, sequential phases. Such processes usually begin with the identification of users' needs and an assessment of the various technological possibilities. Then a detailed set of product specifications is created and, once approved by senior management, is set in stone. At that point, attention shifts to implementation as a functionally integrat-

Marco Iansiti is an associate professor at the Harvard Business School in Boston, Massachusetts, where his research focuses on the factors that influence R&D performance. He is the author of Technology Integration: Making Critical Choices in a Dynamic World, *which will be published by the Harvard Business School Press in the fall of 1997. His last article for HBR was "Technology Integration: Turning Great Research into Great Products" (May-June 1997).* **Alan MacCormack** *is a doctoral candidate in the Technology and Operations Management group at the Harvard Business School. His research explores how companies manage product development in rapidly changing business environments.*

Two Approaches to Product Development

The Traditional Approach

Project Start — Concept Freeze — Market Introduction

Concept Development

Implementation

Concept Time — Response Time

Total Lead Time

The Flexible Approach

Project Start — Concept Freeze — Market Introduction

Concept Development

Implementation

Concept Time — Response Time

Total Lead Time

Speed is a subtle concept in this model. *Total lead time* – the time taken to fulfill the initial objectives of the project – is clearly important; but *concept time* and *response time* are critical measures themselves. Concept time is the window of opportunity for including new information and for optimizing the match between the technology and its application context. Response time is the period during which the window is closed, the product's architecture is frozen, and the project is unable to react to new information. Although the total lead time is the same for both processes above, the flexible process has a shorter response time and is therefore preferable in rapidly changing environments.

formation that arises during the course of a product's development. Systemic changes in a project's definition and basic direction are managed proactively; designers begin this process with no precise idea of how it will end. (See the chart "Two Approaches to Product Development.")

When technology, product features, and competitive conditions are predictable or evolve slowly, a traditional development process works well. But in turbulent business environments, a sequential approach to product development is more than inefficient; it risks creating an obsolete product – one that fails to address customer needs and to make use of the latest technologies. When new competitors and technologies are likely to appear overnight, when standards and regulations are in flux, and when a company's entire customer base can easily switch to other suppliers, businesses don't need a development process that resists change – they need one that embraces it.

A Flexible Process at Work

Not every company interested in developing a flexible product-development process would have to go to the extremes that Netscape did. But by looking at Netscape's experiences, we can see how a highly flexible process works. Founded in 1994, the company pioneered the easy-to-use Web browser: a software interface that provides access to the World Wide Web. The Web browser has transformed the Internet from a communications channel for scientists and technicians into a network connecting millions of ordinary users across time and space – and thus into an industry in its own right.

But Netscape faced no easy task in developing its Web browser, Navigator. In the rapidly evolving Internet industry, many alternative technologies and applications compete for attention, and product development is a project manager's nightmare. The major challenge in the development of a Web

ed team translates the concept into reality. If the up-front work has been done correctly, inherently expensive changes to the product's specifications are kept to a minimum. Indeed, the number of engineering changes is often used as a measure of a project's effectiveness: many changes signify an inferior effort.

In contrast, flexible product development delays until as late as possible any commitment to a final design configuration. The concept development phase and the implementation phase thus overlap instead of following each other sequentially. By accepting the need for and reducing the cost of changes, companies are able to respond to new in-browser is the level of technical complexity involved: a typical program rivals a traditional word processing or spreadsheet application in size, and it must work seamlessly with myriad different hardware and software platforms. The level of uncertainty is so high that even the most basic decisions about a product must be continually revised as new information arises. And the fact that industry giant Microsoft, which had already developed its own flexible product-development process, was readying a product to compete with Navigator only added to the complexity and urgency of Netscape's development effort.

Netscape introduced Navigator 2.0 to the market in January of 1996 and immediately thereafter began to develop the next version of the Web browser, Navigator 3.0, which was to be released in August of the same year. (See the chart "The Development of Navigator 3.0: A Timeline.") The Netscape development group – which included staff from engineering, marketing, and customer support – produced the first prototype quickly. By February 14, just six weeks into the project, it had put a Beta 0 version of the program up on the company's internal project Web site for testing by the development staff. Although many of the intended functions were not yet available, the prototype captured enough of the essence of the new product to generate

meaningful feedback from members of the development group. On February 22, less than two weeks later, the team posed an updated version, Beta 1, again for internal development staff only. In early March, with major bugs in the product worked out, the first public release, Beta 2, appeared on Netscape's Internet Web site. Additional public releases followed thereafter every few weeks until the official release date in August, with gradual refinements appearing in each beta iteration.

The sequence of beta versions was extremely useful to Netscape because it enabled the development team to react both to feedback from users and to changes in the marketplace while the team was still working on the Web browser's design. Beta users by and large are more sophisticated than Netscape's broader customer base and therefore are a valuable source of information. Most useful among them are developers from other Internet

software companies, who tend to be extremely vocal customers. Because many of these customers use the Navigator browser as part of the environment in which their own products operate, they are often the first to find the more complicated bugs – bugs that are revealed only when the product is stretched to the limits of its performance in complex applications.

Getting input from users was one way in which the Navigator team generated new information during the course of the project. During the seven-month development cycle, however, the team also paid careful attention to competing products. As the largest and most powerful software developer in the industry, Microsoft was considered a very serious threat to Netscape's then-dominant position in the browser market. The software giant had just undertaken a dramatic – and very public – switch in strategy, refocusing its formidable talents squarely on the Internet. As a result, Netscape continually monitored the latest beta versions of Microsoft's competing product, Explorer, to compare features and formats. Based on the information that it gathered, the Netscape team would often add format or feature changes to the current beta version of its own product.

In order to respond to the constant stream of new information being brought into the development process, the team carried out extensive experimentation and testing. Subgroups working on individual features went through numerous design-build-test cycles, gradually adding functionality to the product. As features were completed, the team integrated them into the evolving product, then conducted tests to ensure that the new feature did not produce unwanted interactions with other parts of the system. These so-called system builds occurred with increasing frequency as the project progressed; they were performed at least daily in the run-up to the official release.

To facilitate the integration of the vast amounts of information generated during the project, Netscape set up a project Web site on its intranet. The site contained the product's development schedule and specifications, each of which was updated as target dates changed or new features were added. In addition, it contained bulletin boards

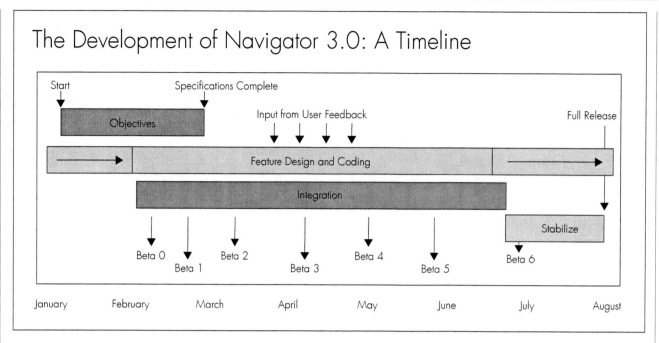

The Development of Navigator 3.0: A Timeline

through which team members could monitor the evolution of various parts of the design, noting the completion of specific features and logging problems in the existing version. Once the Navigator moved to public beta testing, these intranet features became especially valuable because an increasing amount of information then had to be received, classified, and processed.

Netscape built into its product-development process considerable flexibility to respond to changes in market demands and technology. And what is already true of companies in the Internet industry is becoming true of companies elsewhere. Our research on the computer-workstation-and-server industry has shown that there, too, a more flexible process is associated with greater performance. In this environment, companies with a faster response time, as measured from the construction of the first physical prototype to commercial shipping, clearly outperform those with slower response times. The use of sophisticated simulation tools allows teams to work with a virtual prototype for much of the project – in effect, creating a significant overlap between the concept and the design implementation phases.

According to Allen Ward and his colleagues in "The Second Toyota Paradox: How Delaying Decisions Can Make Better Cars Faster" (*Sloan Management Review*, Spring 1995), there also is evidence that a more flexible model has emerged in the automotive industry. Toyota's development process allows it to delay many design decisions until later in the development cycle. The development team creates several sets of design options and, finally,

through a process of elimination, selects only one for implementation. As a result, Toyota can respond to changing market conditions at a later stage than many of its competitors.

The Foundations of a Flexible Process

How should companies create a flexible development process? The experiences of leading companies suggest that senior managers first must understand what gives the process its flexibility. Product development flexibility is rooted in the ability to manage jointly the evolution of a product and its application context. The goal is to capture a rich understanding of customer needs and alternative technical solutions as a project progresses, then to integrate that knowledge into the evolving product design. The faster a project can integrate that information, the faster that project can respond to changes in the product's environment.

The value of flexible product development, however, is only as good as the quality of the process it uses to generate information about the interaction between technical choices and market requirements. Unlike traditional development projects, which rely on periodic bursts of input on users' needs, projects in turbulent business environments require continual feedback. To acquire and use this information, the development process must be able to sense customer needs, to test alternative technical solutions, and to integrate the knowledge gained of both markets and technologies into a coherent product. (See the chart "The Structure of a Flexible Product-Development Process.")

As we describe how leading companies have achieved a more flexible development process, many of the examples we cite come from our work with several software companies that have recently launched Internet products or services. But bear in mind that this is not the only industry in which these lessons apply. We also describe specific practices from other, more traditional industries to illustrate that the approaches used are not unique to the Internet. In fact, they represent cutting-edge practice across a range of environments where change is – or is becoming – the norm.

Sensing the Market. The first element of a flexible process is sensing the needs of customers and the market. Flexible projects establish mechanisms for getting continual feedback from the market on how the evolving design meets customers' requirements. They do so by creating intensive links with the customer base – links that range from broad experimentation with many customers to selective experiences with a few lead users. Furthermore, these customers do not have to be external to the company: leading companies make extensive use of internal staff and resources to provide a test bed for evolving new products.

Gaining continual feedback from customers was particularly critical at Netscape because of its dramatic head-to-head race with Microsoft. Netscape's broad-based release of multiple beta versions to its entire customer base allowed users to play a significant role in the evolving product design. At the same time, it allowed Netscape to test an extremely complex technical product. Although not all Netscape's customers actually experimented with beta versions, the Web browser's most advanced users had to because they themselves were creating

products that needed to work seamlessly with the Navigator release. And their feedback clearly had an impact: a significant portion of the new code, features, and technology that were integrated into the new release was developed only after the first beta version went public.

Microsoft, Netscape's chief rival, was slow to recognize the opportunities offered by the World Wide

Today a rigid, sequential development approach can risk creating an obsolete product.

Web. Not until the end of 1995 did the company begin to focus on developing Internet products. Yet when Bill Gates and the rest of the senior management team finally acknowledged the need for a strategic shift, Microsoft's development expertise was unleashed with astonishing speed. In the six months from the end of 1995 to the middle of 1996, the company went from having no presence in the critical browser market to offering a product that several industry experts claimed was comparable to or better than Netscape's Navigator.

Microsoft was able to react quickly because its existing product-development process had been founded on the rapid iteration of prototypes, early beta releases, and a flexible approach to product architecture and specification. (For a detailed account of Microsoft's development process, see Michael A. Cusumano and Richard W. Selby, *Microsoft Secrets* [Free Press, 1995].) The process that Microsoft followed in developing its Internet Explorer was similar to Netscape's but was more internally oriented. With more than 18,000 employees to Netscape's 1,000 at the time, Microsoft could test successive Explorer beta versions extensively just by putting them up on its own intranet. "Everyone around Microsoft is encouraged to play with it," explained a Microsoft program manager. "Internal testing means that we release it to thousands of people who really hammer away at it. We use the product much more heavily than the average Web user." Microsoft combined broad internal testing by employees with carefully staged external beta releases, using only two or three in contrast to Netscape's six or seven. The company thus limited the risk that imperfections in early releases might damage its reputation.

A similar flexible philosophy can be used in the development of services. Consider Yahoo!. Found-

The Structure of a Flexible Product-Development Process

Sensing the Market

Specification				
Design				
Testing				
Integration				
Stabilization/Ramp-Up				

ed in 1995, the company offers search, directory, and programming services for navigating the World Wide Web. As a service provider, the company believes that before a new offering is released to the outside world, it needs to be more robust than the typical Internet software beta. The market risk of broad, public testing is too high: users who try a new service once and have an unsatisfactory experi-

A flexible approach allows companies to respond to changes in markets and technologies *during* the development cycle.

ence with it either are unlikely to return or, worse, may defect to competitors. Furthermore, Yahoo! assumes that competing companies will copy the innovative features of a new service once it has been released. These factors suggest delaying external testing to late in the development cycle.

For these reasons, Yahoo! puts early versions of new services on-line for internal use only. Given its development team's technical skills and breadth of experience, these trials expose any major technical flaws in the service and provide additional suggestions for improving functionality. Only then does Yahoo! begin a "soft release" of the offering: the service is put up on Yahoo!'s Web site but without any links to highly frequented parts of the site. As a result, only the more technically aggressive users are likely to find and use the service at this stage. Yahoo! also asks some of the 30,000 users, who have volunteered to be beta testers, to try the new service – thus exposing the service to rigorous external testing without revealing it to unsophisticated users who might be frustrated by a slow, incomplete, or error-ridden version.

The Netscape, Yahoo!, and Microsoft examples illustrate several approaches to sensing customer and market needs: broad consumer testing, broad internal testing, and testing by lead users. Companies adopting a flexible development approach should consider the merits of each, as well as the potential for using a balanced combination of all. It is important to emphasize, however, that these techniques are not unique to the Internet. Advances in information technology now allow companies to sense customer needs in ways not possible a few years ago. Leading companies in many industries have begun to use these new capabilities.

Fiat, for example, used a broad, external testing approach, not unlike Netscape's, to evaluate several automobile concepts. A link on the company's Web site directed customers to a page aimed at evaluating users' needs for the next generation of the Fiat Punto, its highest-volume car, which sells about 600,000 units per year. Customers were asked to fill out a survey indicating their preferences in automobile design. They could prioritize the following five considerations: style, comfort, performance, price, and safety. Then they were asked to describe what they hated most in a car and to suggest ideas for new features. Next the software allowed customers to design a car themselves. They could select from a variety of body styles, wheel designs, and styles for the front and rear of the automobile. They also could examine different types of headlights, details, and features. In this way, users could experiment with different designs and see the results immediately on the screen. The software captured the final results; in addition, it traced the sequence that customers went through in evaluating and selecting options. This information told designers much about the logic customers used to evaluate features, styles, and characteristics in order to arrive at a given design solution.

Fiat received more than 3,000 surveys in a three-month period, each comprising about ten pages of detailed information. The ideas suggested ranged from clever (an umbrella holder inside the car) to significant (a single bench front seat). Fiat used the information to inform a variety of styling and concept decisions for the next-generation Punto. And the total cost of the exercise was only $35,000, about the cost of running a few focus groups. Moreover, Fiat executives claimed that the surveys provided them with precisely the data they needed. The profile of the survey's participants – trend-setting individuals with high incomes, who are 31 to 40 years old and frequent car buyers – was the target segment most useful to Fiat.

General Motors' Electro-Motive division has adopted a similar philosophy in its new virtual-product-development process. That process allows engineers to give customers digital tours of next-generation locomotives even as their development proceeds. Although the GM system is still evolving, the aim is to move to an all-digital environment in which the product moves electronically through concept design, analysis, prototyping, and manufacture, and along the way makes several stops on the customer's desktop for feedback.

Testing Technical Solutions. Sensing customer and market needs as a project progresses is one element of a flexible development process. If companies are going to allow a product's design to evolve well into the design implementation phase, however, they also must adopt mechanisms that lower the cost of changes, speed their implementation, and test their impact on the overall system. Such mechanisms allow companies to evaluate and test alternative technical solutions at a rapid rate: the second element of a flexible development process.

Early prototypes and tests of alternative technologies are critical to establishing the direction of a project. Consider NetDynamics, a company that develops sophisticated tools for linking Web servers to large databases. The single most important technical decision confronting NetDynamics during the development of its second product release was the early choice of language in its product. Either the company could develop a proprietary language, or it could use Java. At that time, in early 1996, the Java programming language had received a lot of publicity, but it was still highly unstable, relatively immature, and little understood. "We knew Java was going to be big," recalled chief engineer Yarden Malka, "but it was still only available as a Beta 1 version. This meant that the development tools that went along with it were either terribly buggy or nonexistent. If we chose it, we knew we also had to develop many of our own tools."

NetDynamics' commitment to an open platform tended to favor Java. If there was a standard – either existing or emerging – it should be used, and Java appeared to be that standard. To make the decision, however, NetDynamics' engineers spent considerable time experimenting with various options, trying to become as comfortable as possible with the benefits and risks of each language. They began by developing simple prototypes and gradually migrated to more complex programs, attempting to gauge the advantages each would give the user. This "user-centric" approach to prototyping and experimentation was critical to the final choice and stands in stark contrast to the approach often adopted by high-tech companies in which technologies often are evaluated purely on the basis of the advantages they give the design team.

As a project progresses, the design team must have the capacity to evaluate and test alternative design solutions quickly and cheaply. Yahoo! can easily do just that because of the way it has elected to provide its Internet service. The company meets its processing needs with many inexpensive computers instead of a few large (and expensive) servers. The small investment required for each machine allows Yahoo! to scale up its capacity smoothly to meet new demand. It also means that Yahoo! can easily run experiments to test different design options. According to Farzad Nazem, the vice president of engineering, "Our Web site setup works just like a spigot valve. If we want to test out a new product or feature on several thousand users, we promote it on the home page of only a few machines. As users access the service and we reach the required volume, we can turn off the promotion on each machine. We can also conduct comparative experiments by running multiple versions of the same service on different computers in the network, then track the results to see which version attracts more customers."

To reduce the cost of testing alternative design choices, companies outside the software industry increasingly have invested in new technologies for virtual design. By designing and testing product designs through simulation, for example, companies achieve the flexibility to respond to new information and to resolve uncertainties by quickly exploring alternatives. Computer-aided design software also has dramatically reduced the cost of design changes, while at the same time speeding up experimentation. At Boeing, for example, the all-digital development of the 777 aircraft made use of a computer-generated "human" who would climb inside the three-dimensional design on-screen to show how difficult maintenance access would be for a live mechanic. Such computer modeling allowed engineers to spot design errors – say, a navigation light that would have been difficult to service – that otherwise would have remained undiscovered until a person negotiated a physical prototype. By avoiding the time and cost associated with building physical prototypes at several stages, Boeing's development process has acquired the flexibility to evaluate a wider range of design options than was previously possible.

Integrating Customer Needs with Technical Solutions. It's no good knowing what customers want in a product under development if the development team can't integrate that information with the available technical solutions. As a result, all the organizations we discuss have established dynamic

Using a flexible development process, Team New Zealand produced a superior yacht– and beat its U.S. opponent.

integration mechanisms. Some of them are based on well-understood concepts, such as using dedicated teams–an approach adopted by Netscape, NetDynamics, and Microsoft. Others are less traditional. All three companies, for example, use their intranets to integrate tasks, synchronize design changes, and capture customer information as projects evolve. Thus project teams are able to keep track of the evolving relationships among tasks, schedules, and design changes in a dynamic way. Such integrating mechanisms are essential for managing a flexible process, given the many rounds of experimentation and the wide range of information generated. Without a way of capturing and integrating knowledge, the development process can quickly dissolve into chaos, with ad hoc design changes creating masses of rework because of unanticipated interactions with other components in the system.

In the Internet world, integrating mechanisms are dictated by the nature of the product–software. Each of the projects we describe adopted sophisticated design-integration tools to hold the master version of the emerging product. As team members went to work on individual components, they checked out the code for that part of the system. Once finished, they had to run a series of tests to ensure that the component did not create problematic interactions with the rest of the system. Only then could they check in the new component. At the end of each day, when all the new components had been checked in, engineers ran the program. Any problems that occurred had to be corrected before new code could be permanently integrated.

Similar approaches are found in projects outside the Internet world where new information systems allow companies to share knowledge more effectively. At Silicon Graphics, a leading manufacturer of workstations and servers, a new product-introduction process makes extensive use of the company's intranet to coordinate development activities. Managers and engineers throughout the world, who respond daily to the problems of current customers, provide input during the concept-generation stage.

In addition, lead users in target application segments (referred to as "lighthouse" customers) are linked directly to the development teams, allowing the teams to get fast and effective guidance on critical decisions as the project evolves. The intranet also is used to integrate design tasks on a daily basis. Project engineers work from a shared body of software that simulates the hardware design. As with the Internet projects, when team members want to make a change, they check out the relevant code, make the desired design improvements, test it for errors and unanticipated interactions, then check it back in.

Such approaches are not limited to high-technology products. Booz Allen & Hamilton, a management consulting firm, approaches the problem of integrating a diverse and geographically dispersed knowledge base by using its intranet. The intranet allows consulting staff quickly to locate and contact industry experts with specific skills and to identify previous studies that are relevant to current projects. In this way, the collective experience of the organization is available to all employees online. The intranet also allows the company to develop its intellectual capital. In management consulting, new-product development consists of developing new frameworks, industry best practices, performance benchmarks, and other information that can be applied across projects. By having these products on-line during development and thereafter, Booz Allen can integrate new information and experiences into its knowledge base.

Integrating within the company, however, is not always sufficient. In some cases, the ability to integrate knowledge across networks of organizations may also be important. For Internet software companies, given the novelty and complexity inherent in their products and the rapidity of their development cycles, no single organization can research, make, and market products alone. Instead, they take advantage of technical possibilities that are beyond the boundaries of any individual company; those technologies can then be integrated into their own core products. (Internet users will be familiar with Java applets and Web browser plug-ins.) Doing so, however, means that just as the technologies must be seamlessly integrated into a product, so must the organization accommodate a changing cast of players. The companies we describe have built alliances with third-party developers, engaged in joint development projects, and worked hard to foster open product architectures and modular designs. And such arrangements are not peculiar to software. Workstation manufacturers such as Sun, Hewlett-Packard, and Silicon Graphics frequently engage in joint development efforts with other hardware companies (such as Siemens, Intel, Fujitsu, Toshiba, and NEC) to leverage the performance of their systems.

Putting Flexibility to the Test

In combination, the foundations of a flexible product-development process allow a company to respond to changes in markets and technologies *during* the development cycle. We found a striking example of how that is done in a setting that is about as far from the typical high-tech world as one can get: the America's Cup. In 1995, a small team from New Zealand dominated the races from start to finish. Team New Zealand's effort shows how the mechanisms we have described can be combined to dramatic effect in a flexible process.

Team New Zealand recruited Doug Peterson, who had been on the winning America's Cup team in 1992, as its lead designer. It also recruited an experienced simulation team to make use of advanced design software. Although Peterson's extensive experience drove the initial concept design, once the team's yachts were constructed the emphasis shifted to evaluating design changes through thousands of computer-simulated design iterations. The simulations were run on a small network of workstations located a few feet from the dock. To ensure rapid feedback on the performance of design changes, the team built two boats. Each day, one of them was fitted with a design change for evaluation; then the two boats raced each other to gauge the impact of the change.

Team New Zealand's flexible process sensed "market needs" through the two-boat testing program, which generated feedback each day on how

the evolving design fit the racing environment. It tested alternative designs through a simulation program that was directed by one of the world's most experienced yacht designers. And it integrated knowledge by making the resulting information available locally. The crew, design team, and management were therefore able to make suggestions for the design, to see the impact of potential changes, and to know what to expect when those changes were tested on the water.

The U.S. boat that Team New Zealand faced in the final race had been designed on the latest supercomputers with the support of large, well-heeled corporations. Although the U.S. team could test a massive number of experimental designs, the computers were located hundreds of miles from the dock. As a result, there were significant delays between detailing a design and getting feedback on results. Furthermore, the team had only one boat on which to test design changes; given the varying sea and wind conditions, it took far longer than its rival to verify the impact of a change.

Team New Zealand's approach had better mechanisms than its U.S. rival for sensing, testing, and integrating what it had learned. Its flexible process produced a yacht of superior design, which many observers believed to be a full generation ahead of its competitors' boats. As Paul Cayard, skipper of Team New Zealand's opponent in the final race, remarked, "I've been in some uphill battles in my life. But I've never been in a race where I felt I had so little control over the outcome. It's the largest discrepancy in boat speed I've ever seen."

We have seen a similar pattern throughout many environments we have studied. Organizations that have adopted a flexible product-development process have begun to transform the very industries that forced them to adopt it. They have implemented strategies that companies clinging to traditional approaches cannot follow. Competitors without flexible development processes will almost certainly find their industries growing more and more turbulent in appearance. And in such an environment, their products and services will always seem to be one step behind those of their more flexible rivals.

Reprint 97505   To place an order, call 800-988-0886.

NEW PRODUCT TEAM LEARNING:
DEVELOPING AND PROFITING FROM YOUR KNOWLEDGE CAPITAL

(G. S. Lynn / #CMR126 / 21 p)

Summary

This article explores organizational learning for new-product development through a study of thirteen innovation teams from Apple, IBM, and Hewlett-Packard. There are, the author explains, three types of team learning: within-team learning, cross-team learning, and market learning. A new-product team need not excel at all three. In fact, in some circumstances certain types of learning can actually be detrimental to a project's outcome.

Outline

Findings
Cost Reduction
New Market Model
Technology Entrepreneur
New Venture Unit
Conclusions

Learning Objectives

- Understand four key types of innovation
- Understand three types of new-product team learning and the proper management of them

Questions, Ideas, and Exercises

1. Consider the four product-team learning strategies identifed in Figure 2 (and explained in the text below this figure). The key challenge in picking the right type of team learning begins with properly characterizing the type of innovation you are seeking to achieve. But note how some of the projects the author describes were undermined by an incorrect characterization of the innovation goal, or a midguided re-characterization in mid-project. Clearly, establishing the depth of innovation you are seeking to achieve in a new product is both critically important and, in many cases, a far from simple matter. If you are working on a new product team at the moment, how confident are you that your company genuinely understands the level of innovation you are seeking to achieve?

2. The author argues that excluding inappropriate types of learning from a new-product team can be an important element in the team's success. But excluding one particular type of learning might be achievable only if the team is virtually segregated from the main culture of the company. How feasible is this in the context of your company's

culture? And how comfortable would you feel taking part in it? Note the author's characterization of the social-psychological effects that Apple Corporation's segregated "Lisa" team had on the rest of the company. While the Lisa debacle is less an indictment of segregated teams than a mandate for using common sense in managing them, it does issue a cautionary warning about the lack of perspective that can occur in segregated teams -- and the organizational fallout that can result.

3. If you are on a new-product team that is concluding its mission, find a systematic way to capture the learning the team has done -- don't assume it will simply be embodied for all to see in the new product. Many books on teams can give you guidance in this regard.

New Product Team Learning:

DEVELOPING AND PROFITING FROM YOUR KNOWLEDGE CAPITAL

Gary S. Lynn

California Management Review **Reprint Series**

©1998 by The Regents of the University of California

CMR, Volume 40, Number 4, Summer 1998

New Product Team Learning:

DEVELOPING AND PROFITING FROM YOUR KNOWLEDGE CAPITAL

Gary S. Lynn

C ontinuous improvement has been credited with helping companies in decreasing manufacturing costs, reducing inventory, compressing cycle time, improving quality, speeding distribution, and increasing customer satisfaction. But what is at the heart of continuous improvement? What allows a company to get better over time? The answer is "learning"—or, more accurately, organizational learning. How effectively an organization learns can dictate whether it will improve, and how fast, or if it is destined to lose ground to competitors who can and do learn.

Nowhere is organizational learning more critical than in new product development, where one technological platform can lead to families of products, and learning must be transferred from one team to the next. Some companies excel at transporting knowledge between teams and then capitalizing on it, while others do not. Motorola built on its portable pager business to develop portable cellular telephones, Searle built on its technical core competency in drug research to develop NutraSweet, and Corning used its expertise in glass technology to develop optical fibers.[1] Xerox, however, failed to apply its copier technology to the personal copier market until competitors were firmly entrenched, Firestone and Goodyear resisted the shift to radial tires, and Seagate waited to develop 3.5" computer disk-drives until other companies had secured an insurmountable lead.[2]

This research would not have been possible without the support we received from the Center for Innovation Management Studies (CIMS) at Lehigh University and the Marketing Science Institute (MSI). Also, this research benefited from the input provided by Barry Bayus, Annie Brooks, Tracy Collins, Peter Koen, Victoria Marsick, Karen McGill, Joseph Morone, Parry Norling, Steven Schnaars, Stanley Slater, Andrew Van de Ven, Calhoun Wick and the participation of numerous new product team members from Apple, IBM, and HP.

Why are some companies able to build competitive advantages by using their storehouse of organizational knowledge while others are not? What programs can companies institute that would enable them to create and profit from the knowledge that they have labored to acquire? How can organizations establish policies enabling their new product teams to draw on the firm's knowledge base, augment it, and then develop the kind of technological breakthroughs that can create entirely new industries?

By studying a progression of new product projects, we learned how teams learn. These projects included the Apple II, IIe, III, Lisa, Mac, and Mac+; the Hewlett-Packard 85, 125, 150, and Vectra; and the IBM DataMaster, PC, and PCjr.[3] The insights came after completing over 85 hours of interviews with 70 team members (19 IBM team members; 25 HP team members; and 26 Apple team members). Interviewees included senior company executives such as Apple's co-founder, Steve Wozniak; HP's Executive Vice President, Dick Hackborn; HP's Personal Computer Office Division General Manger, Bob Puette; and IBM's initial PC project leader, Bill Lowe, in addition to managers and individual team members in manufacturing, marketing, planning, and engineering (hardware, software, and firmware).[4]

Findings

What we found was that learning was critical to the successes and lacking in the failures. We also uncovered not one but three different forms of team learning. The first is called Within-Team Learning and is the learning that occurs within the context of the team itself. Within-Team Learning can be characterized as learning by doing. The experience curve in continuous process innovation is a classic example. The second form of learning, called Cross-Team Learning, is the experience gained by one team within a company and then transplanted to another. Boeing, for example, relied on Cross-Team Learning when it compiled "Project Homework"—a program designed to capture the lessons it had learned on the 707, 727, 737, and 747 teams and then applied that knowledge in developing the successful 757 and 767.[5] The third form of learning, called Market Learning, is the knowledge gained external to the firm—from competitors, suppliers, and customers. Sun Microsystems, for example, relied on Market Learning to uncover the advantages and disadvantages of competitive products and technologies. With this information, the company was able to use primarily off-the-shelf components, including a Motorola processor and champion the open architecture workstation, a strategy that propelled the company past all others including Apollo, the market pioneer.[6]

Team Learning Strategies

Under what circumstances are Within-Team, Cross-Team, and Market Learning needed? Must new product teams excel in all three? After we analyzed all the cases, this question vexed us. There did not seem to be a consistent

FIGURE 1. Innovation Environments[8]

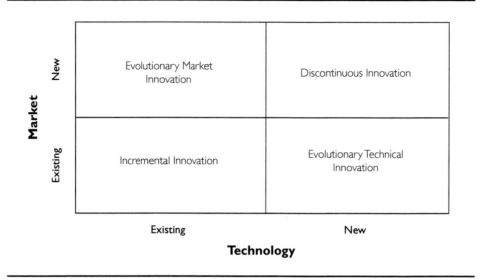

learning pattern across projects even after comparing and contrasting the successful projects to the not-so-successful ones.[7] However, after we segmented the projects according to the degree of technical and market uncertainty,[8] different learning mechanisms and strategies became apparent. Ironically, teams do not need to excel at all three forms of learning. Some learning strategies can actually be detrimental to a new product development effort. Team learning strategies must be tailored to a given innovation.

The upper right quadrant of Figure 1 (where the technology as well as the market are new to the innovating firm) represents the most extreme form of innovation and poses severe challenges to the new product professional. When a company is attempting to develop and commercialize discontinuous innovations that are targeted to new markets as well as new technologies that are outside the company's core competencies, learning mechanisms must focus on developing and refining fresh market, technical, and economic models that are needed to compete. The current models used by the company can be inappropriate, and even counter-productive in this new environment. As a result, teams trying to develop these discontinuous innovations must shed some of the organizational baggage that the company has previously acquired. A company trying to launch these New Technology/New Market products would be analogous to the adage of teaching an old dog new tricks. To accomplish this form of learning, teams must restrict Cross-Team Learning by forming a New Venture Unit—an autonomous group with adequate authority and resources—because teams must be free to break with tradition. Teams must not be encumbered with corporate axioms such as, "We have always done it that way, and will continue to do it that way." As a result, Cross-Team Learning plays a restricted role. Within-Team

Learning, on the other hand is critical. This form of learning allows the insights gained by one team member to be shared with others on the team. Market Learning plays a somewhat limited role because the customers are unfamiliar with these innovations and would have a difficult time verbalizing their needs. If, for example, in 1975, you had surveyed executives about their need to have a personal computer on their desk, the answer would almost certainly have been negative. The popular strategy of listening to the "voice of the customer" would have been misleading. Although Market Learning from customers can be misleading for discontinuous innovation, learning from competitors can be helpful. Steve Wozniak, who was the chief designer on both the Apple I and II, benefited from Market Learning—he immersed himself in computers. Wozniak would send away for computer schematics of all types. And once he received the schematics, he would study them. His design of the I and II were greatly influenced from analyzing the strengths and weaknesses of other computers.

Organizational Team Learning Mechanisms in Practice

Apple Computer is known for producing a series of discontinuous innovations including the Apple II, III, and Lisa personal computers. As history, in July 1976, Apple Computer launched its Apple I "computer," which was essentially a printed circuit board that sold for $666.66. The Apple I was followed in April 1977, by the Apple II. The Apple II was the first personal computer with color graphics capability and retailed for $1,300 without a monitor (it was to be attached to a home television set). The system was powered by a 6502 CPU with 4K of RAM. The Apple II was developed by a small, close-knit team of people who worked out of a cramped garage, and later from in a single-room office with severely limited capital. The Apple II team followed the 1/10th rule: You can get by on 1/10th the funds if you are willing to work ten times as hard. It seemed to work. The Apple II was enormously successful. In its first nine months, 4,000 Apple IIs were sold. By 1979, this number increased to 35,000 and, by February 1983, to 30,000 units per month.[9] During June 1983, the millionth Apple II rolled off the assembly line.

The overall objectives of the Apple II were clear and shared among the small team. The vision of the Apple II was to build a product that team members themselves would want and use. Steve Wozniak, Apple's co-founder and the chief designer of the Apple II explains:

> I did have a strong vision that it [the Apple II] should be very nice-looking and powerful-looking. It should approach you like a human in its shape. I was after simple things that were powerful—that were show-offable, that could do fun things for people. I wanted a real human approach to a computer. Not "it's a computer that can run equipment at my company," or something. I was after just a human use: games, and the ability to let me run a couple of small programs to solve circuit problems at HP. That was my other goal. So I had a real simple direction of what I wanted

The Apple II put Apple Computer on the map and set the stage for the personal computer revolution. The Apple II gave way to several successful as well as not-so-successful personal computer innovations by Apple. Following the Apple II came the Apple III and Apple IIe. These computers were designed as product improvements and extensions of the Apple II. The Lisa, Mac, and Mac+ also followed and were mouse-driven, used a graphical-user-interface, and represented a new approach to personal computers.

The Lisa and the Apple II employed new technologies, and both were targeted to new markets. The Lisa was launched in January 1983, and in several aspects was similar to the Apple II. However, Lisa was strikingly different in many other ways. The Lisa project was similar to the Apple II in that both were substantial technological advancements at the time: the Apple II with its integrated design and floppy disk drive, and the Lisa with its mouse-based, graphical user interface (GUI). Both teams were also isolated—the Apple II because there was no other Apple teams at the time, and the Lisa because team members were housed in a separate location and accessible only to people with specially-issued Lisa security badges. The teams were different in their respective sizes—the Apple II had a core team of from two to ten people in the early stages compared to the 50-60 members on the Lisa team. Furthermore, the teams differed in their respective composition. The Apple II was primarily composed of "computer" hobbyists, whereas the Lisa team was composed of formally trained industrial-computer engineers. The chief engineer, Wayne Rosing, came from DEC along with four other DEC people; 18 programmers came from HP; and one engineer came from Xerox PARC where the mouse technology was pioneered.[10] The two teams also differed in their physical quarters and in the amount of resources available. The Apple II team was housed in an old garage, whereas the Lisa team had plush offices with skylights and plants throughout. Taylor Pohlman, the Apple II Product Marketing Manager, recalls the Lisa offices as "the most luxurious place we'd [the Apple II team] ever seen; and we were living in this armpit." The Lisa team spared no expense in its offices or on the project in general. The lavishness backfired on the Lisa team because with so many people with seemingly inexhaustible resources, the vision of the Lisa grew virtually unimpeded. The Lisa team tried to do too much. Randy Battat who was the Product Marketing Manager on the Lisa project explains:

> Maybe the Lisa vision was too broad, but it was trying to break some paths. It was tackling so many brand new fundamental things all at the same time: applications, operating systems, and hardware. The aspirations were to build the equivalent of a mid-range minicomputer into a desk-top box and change the paradigm at the same time and have a fully robust UNIX-like operating system and write seven new applications from scratch and custom design floppy disc drives, custom design hard disc drives, etc. So I think the fundamental problem with Lisa was, if the vision was too broad, it was because there was so much resource thrown at the thing that one did not have to make trade-offs.

The broad vision created problems and dissension within the group because team members did not have clear idea of what they were trying to do. The overreaching goal of Lisa was be an office productivity tool, but an office productivity tool can be anything from a fax machine to a ruler. As a result, team members did not agree on what the vision of the Lisa was supposed to be nor what it was supposed to do. Over time, the features and functionality of the Lisa grew, and with it, so did the cost. What began as a $2,000, 8-bit computer, became a $9,995, 16-bit computer. Unfortunately, the market was not ready for a $10,000 personal computer; sales for the first year fell woefully below forecast. The first year Lisa forecast called for 1983 sales to reach 50,000 units, but only 11,000 units were actually sold.[11] Repeated attempts to revive the Lisa failed, and in April 1985, at an Apple Board meeting, the Lisa was canceled and dropped entirely.

As an interesting comparison to Apple, Hewlett-Packard tried repeatedly to crack the PC market. Finally, after 12 years of trials and setbacks, HP was able to achieve the success it had sought. HP is frequently cited as one of the most outstanding companies and one of the best to work for. Why did HP take so long to figure out how to compete in PCs? Why did HP have to launch four personal computer product lines (the HP85, HP125, HP150, and early Vectra) to finally figure out the formula for success? Ironically, HP's past learning—a heritage and culture developed over the prior 30 to 40 years—detracted from its ability to successfully compete in this emerging market. HP had figured out a formula for success in its other businesses: instruments, calculators, and minicomputers. HP's past experience and learning served as core rigidities hindering the company's ability to win in the PC marketplace.[12]

As background, in 1980, HP launched is first "personal computer," called the HP85, which came out of HP's calculator division. It sold for $3,250 and had a 40-character 5" CRT screen, with up to 32K of RAM, a tape storage drive, and a thermal printer. The unit was compact and portable because it was designed by many of the same people who developed the HP35 and HP65 portable calculators. Unfortunately, the size and weight design parameters of the HP85 limited its performance and functionality. Although a 5" screen was large for a calculator, it severely restricted the HP85's use as a personal computer.

During this time, the PC market was growing, but it was not clear to HP engineers nor to their marketers what a personal computer should be or to whom it should be targeted. A formal market and technical analysis of Apple and other personal computer companies was never conducted. As a result, the initial vision for the HP85 was somewhat unclear to team members. As Dan Terpack, the Division Marketing Manager for the HP85 recalls:

> Clarity wasn't there. I think fuzzy is the right word. You have to put it in the context of that time frame where there was talk about PCs, but not a lot of agreement to it.

As the HP85 project progressed, Bob Watson, who had a background in instrument controllers for HP, was brought in as the new divisional manager. When Watson learned about the HP85 and its capabilities, he thought that with minor alterations including adding plug-in interface ports and a more convenient numeric entry keypad, the HP85 could be used as an equipment controller (e.g., to turn a piece of equipment on or off). The team agreed to implement Watson's changes and to simultaneously pursue the controller market with the HP85. The HP85 achieved success as a controller by capitalizing on existing HP sales force. As a controller, the HP85 could be sold through existing channels of distribution to current scientific customers. But as a PC that required new channels and customers, the HP85 fell short in both sales and profit expectations.

After the launch of the HP85, HP's other divisions began dabbling in the PC market. HP's Computer Systems Division (CSD), the division responsible for minicomputers and terminals, developed a product called the HP125. The HP125 was launched in August 1981, one day before IBM launched its PC. The HP125 was built on the CSD's heritage in the minicomputer and terminal businesses. The result was a product designed to function as both a terminal as well as a personal computer; the HP125 had a split personality. The HP125's two-pronged vision was primarily the byproduct of the close, intra-divisional, cross-pollination and cross-team communication that occurred among people within CSD. However, there was little inter-divisional communication between the HP125 and HP85 teams. Bob Puette, the Personal Computer Office Division General Manager (the division responsible for the HP125) describes the relationship between divisions as, "more like a street fight." As a result, the HP125 team did not learn from the mistakes that the HP85 team had made. When the HP125 was launched, it was an under-powered, 8-bit personal computer with an over-powered, over-priced terminal. The HP125 ran CPM's operating system and was powered by two Z-80 microprocessors—one to control the PC and one for the terminal emulator. The HP125, as both a computer as well as a terminal, fell far short in sales and profit projections.

HP tried to correct its mistakes on the HP125, and CSD launched the HP150 in September 1983. However, because the HP150 team was also part of the terminal business, when the new PC was developed it also had a split personality. It was again both a personal computer and a terminal emulator. Although the HP150 met with limited success in the terminal market and despite several innovations such as a 9" touch-screen monitor and a 3.5" floppy drive (a first at the time), the HP150 was unsuccessful in establishing any significant foothold in the PC market. Reasons for the failure of the HP150 as a PC were that the HP150 team had two mentalities etched in its genetic makeup. The first was the HP150 team's heritage in the terminal business, and the second was the mindset within HP to innovate—to make a substantial technical contribution. Despite a study by consulting companies for HP indicating the need for being fully IBM compatible, the idea of being an IBM clone maker was repugnant to most engineers on the HP150 project. Larry Kelly, the HP125 and HP150 R&D Lab Manager explains the HP design mentality:

> HP has this very strong, "not invented here" syndrome. Most of the time it's good. In the computer industry, it's hard to apply. The test always used to be, when you had an idea or were working on a project, what's the contribution? What have you done that nobody's done before? That [mentality] works fine for instruments but that's in direct contrast with being compatible. So you've got a company that's 35 or 40 years old at the time with $1 or $2 billion in revenue. And, you've got all these engineers thinking, "You can't wear your boots unless you know you've done something nobody else's done—you can't come to work." Overcoming that mentality was very hard. It took them [HP engineers up to its senior management] four or five years to realize that it [an HP PC] had to be compatible [with IBM] first and then maybe you could innovate after that.

After the disappointing results of the HP150, HP again tried to correct its mistakes and developed its Vectra personal computer. This time, senior management reorganized the divisional reporting structure and moved the PC group out of the terminal division. As a result, when the Vectra was launched in September 1985, it was not a terminal emulator; it was exclusively a PC. Also, HP was learning about the channels of distribution needed to compete in personal computers markets. The HP sales force that was used to calling on major accounts and selling minicomputers for $100,000 was inappropriate for selling a $3,199 to $5,399 PC. Nonetheless, HP could not shed its innovative mind-set. Its engineers opposed launching a clone of IBM. Thus when the Vectra was finally launched, it was not fully IBM compatible. Once again consulting companies were hired to assist HP with its marketing strategy, but as Jim Carlson, Vectra's Marketing Manager recalls:

> I don't know if the consulting companies said it, but we did not hear them say that the Vectra had to be *totally* IBM compatible.

The Vectra limped along for eight years selling 8,000-10,000 units per month, well below its competitors' PCs, which included IBM, Apple, and Compaq. Finally, almost 15 years after its first entrance into the PC market, HP learned how to compete and succeed. In April 1992, HP shipped approximately 9,000 units, but 15 months later, they were shipping 70,000 units per month. In 1995 and 1996, HP's PC volume surpassed 150,000 units per month, and by 1996, the company had risen to the number three position in domestic PC sales and number one in several foreign countries. How were they able to turn their PC business around? The change happened largely because HP was finally able to shed its organizational baggage. Senior management reorganized the personal computer division and combined it with peripheral products (including laser printers) under the auspices of Dick Hackborn. Hackborn was the executive who in less than ten years had helped establish HP as the world's leading supplier of small personal printers. The peripheral division was the perfect home for HP's line of PCs because peripherals (such as laser printers) were being sold through computer dealers, which was the same channel needed for the PC. People in the peripheral business understood the business model needed to compete in the PC dealer marketplace. By the mid-1980s, the Vectra had moved to the lower left quadrant of Figure 1; and people such as Hackborn had learned what it took to succeed in an existing market with an existing technology—improve cycle time, reduce cost by lowering overhead, and price competitively. These were bedrock strategies for the laser printer business. Consequently, when Hackborn was given responsibility for the personal computer division, he used the laser-printer business model. Hackborn describes his strategy:

> I think [personal computers] were just in the wrong part of the company. They were using the wrong business models for the business. If you just move them to the next adjoining railroad track—that was the printers—they were an entirely different management team. And it was much closer to the business model that they needed to compete. I think that just took a long time to happen at HP.

Once this new business model was instituted, it was accepted by most of the people working on the Vectra Program. As Tom Buiocchi, the Vectra Product Marketing Manager recalls:

> One of [Bob] Frankenburg's [who became HP's PC General Manager] best lines was, "let's make new mistakes, let's price too low for a while and see what happens." It was really great rallying call for a lot of the folks in marketing. We had been waiting for this [a new strategy] for eight years. We were waiting for the go ahead—the license to compete. Once we got it, we knew what to do. Until that point, we were almost shackled by the focus on HP internally connected products, the direct sales force, and sometimes by having to price at a premium.

International Business Machines, like HP, had its share of failures. The DataMaster program, the precursor to the IBM PC, began in February 1978 and was to be an inexpensive computer geared to small businesses. The DataMaster was launched in July 1981, but became obsolete in just a few months. The Data-Master was an 8-bit computer that used an Intel 8085 microprocessor with 32K of RAM (expandable to 128K), a 12" monochrome monitor with options that included two 8" floppy disk drives, a 30 MB hard disk drive and a printer. The price for the unit without floppies, hard disk drive, or printer was $3,300; with the floppy drives and a printer, it sold for $9,830. IBM's management had hoped that the DataMaster would lead to a family of products over the course of five years or more, but it never did.

Why did the DataMaster fail? One of the reasons was because the Data-Master objectives—the "rules of the game"—changed during the course of its development, which delayed the program and confused the team. The original vision of the DataMaster was an open-architecture computer that small businesses could use and that would run off-the-shelf, third-party software. Unfortunately, senior IBM management changed the direction midway into the project and required that the DataMaster be a closed-architecture system and be compatible with other IBM computers. This change in focus meant that DataMaster customers would have to write their own custom software because off-the-shelf programs would most likely be incompatible with the machine. This changed the target market from small businesses to medium-sized businesses who had the resources to commission custom programs. Small businesses (such as automobile repair shops and insurance agencies) would no longer be viable markets because of the high cost of custom programs.

Furthermore, although the DataMaster was allowed to use a vendor supplied microprocessor, a major departure from IBM's normal protocol, the team was relegated to purchasing all components through the company's traditional channel, the Corporate Architecture Committee (CAC), which had absolute rights over any components that IBM procured. The CAC had to qualify all components used in an IBM computer and by the time the CAC got through with their testing and qualifying, the price escalated and the time required to procure a component increased dramatically. Lew Eggebrecht, the DataMaster Architect Design Team Leader, recalls some of the problems encountered on the DataMaster:

> We had a product, but the product definition got changed over time with the DataMaster. The original functions of the DataMaster were correct because they were the same assumptions the [IBM] PC was built under—outside technology, outside software, quick development, a very cohesive small team, use of industry standards for software and hardware. All of those things, or a large portion of them changed on the DataMaster.

The net results were mid-course changes, delays, cost overruns and performance limitations, all of which doomed the DataMaster. But was the Data-Master truly unsuccessful? As Dave Bradley, an Advisory Engineer on the DataMaster, describes it, "I've always characterized the DataMaster as IBM learning how not to do something." The DataMaster set the stage for IBM's development of the PC.

Most of us know the story of the IBM PC, how it was developed in record time for IBM (13 months) and that it was incredibly successful. However, the PC was not a discontinuous innovation; the market was new for IBM but the technology was not. Several innovations succeeded the PC: the XT, AT, and PCjr. The XT and AT were incremental innovations, but the PCjr. not only included new technologies (such as an infrared keyboard that did not need a cable, as well as a plug-in cartridge storage system for games and software programs), but it also was targeted to a new market—the home market. To reach this new market, the PCjr. would have to be sold through new channels that included department stores such as K-Mart and Sears—unfamiliar markets for IBM. The PCjr. was a discontinuous innovation and it was based on an Intel 8088 microprocessor, had 64K of RAM and a 5¼" floppy drive selling for $1,300.

Unfortunately, the PCjr. did not achieve anywhere near the level of success of its predecessor, the PC. Market reaction to PCjr. was highly critical of the keyboard, the plug-in cartridge, as well as other performance and compatibility limitations. Potential customers as well as magazine reviewers were expecting another home run like the PC, but the PCjr. merely hit a single.

Why did the PCjr. fail so soundly despite the lessons learned from the PC? Why was IBM unable to transfer its learning from the PC project to the PCjr.? In the first place, the people on the PC team had to be spread across all three projects, the XT, AT, and PCjr. As a result, there was simply not enough critical mass of technical and market expertise to serve all three projects. Bill Sydnes, the PCjr. System Manager (the overall project manager), was required to hire people from the Series 1 minicomputer program (because they "were around" at a time when that product was being phased out), instead of using experienced PC people and peppering them with new recruits who had fire in their bellies (as did the PC Program). Sydnes explains:

> I was directed on the Jr. that, "You will first hire people from the Boca Raton site." We should have never done that. They [people available at Boca] were Series 1 guys who had backgrounds in IBM technology and methodologies. They were your typical 9-4 guys. They had very inappropriate skill sets. I would have liked to have not been constrained. I didn't need them from the PC team. I needed the ability to hire people who were not in the IBM mold. I wasn't constrained like that on the PC.

Another reason for the disappointing performance of the PCjr. was that midway into the program, senior management changed the objectives and ignored one of the critical lessons learned from the DataMaster: not to change the vision—the blueprint. The initial vision of the PCjr. was a powerful, versatile, home/game computer for personal use, but senior management disagreed. As a result, a vision conflict persisted. Sydnes recalls how the team's position differed from management's position:

> The Jr. was originally intended to have a large number of peripherals on it that would have allowed it to compete at the low end of the PC product line. It would have obliterated the low end of the PC product line. IBM's position was, "We're not going to allow you to do that."

Further complicating the blurred vision on the PCjr. was a conflict in the degree of compatibility needed between the PCjr. and the PC. Initially, the Jr. was to be given a clean sheet of paper, allowing the team to design the best home computer it could, independent of compatibility. But, as the project progressed, senior management changed the rules and the vision and required the PCjr. to be fully compatible with the PC. Why was management allowed to change the vision on the PCjr. but not on the PC? Because the PCjr. team was only partially autonomous. It was forced to share marketing and finance personnel with the other PC teams. These people had shared loyalties. Meanwhile, another dynamic was unfolding: IBM was having second thoughts about selling a home/game computer. They were concerned about being perceived as a home computer company. After all, the company's name was International "Business"

Machines; not International "Home" Machines. As David O'Connor, who took over from Sydnes as the PCjr.'s System Manger, recalls:

> There were some guys at the top of the corporation who really, really believed that they didn't want the IBM logo in the retail or consumer distribution channel at that time. "IBM is not a consumer company. They're a business company. They sell to professionals and businesses and large corporations; this home computer stuff is not for us." The instant there was any problem with the program, it gave those who felt IBM should not be in that market a lot of reason to suggest that we delay the program.

What began as a new venture unit quickly changed to include a high degree of involvement from top management. Senior management came in and altered the rules. They required that the PCjr. be: fully compatible with the PC; de-functionalized so not to cannibalize the low-end of the PC market; and geared to both the home as well as the business markets. The result of mid-course changes was that Sydnes left. His leaving created a void that was difficult to fill. Gary Pitt, the Engineering Manager on the PCjr., describes the impact of Sydnes departure:

> A lot of the ideas we were incorporating into the design [on the PCjr.] were Sydnes'. I think much of it was in Sydnes head and left with him. Bill [Sydnes] had fundamental input on the initial designs. They were his concepts. It was his baby. He had an ownership that was lost when he left.

Not only did the overall project management change, but when Dave O'Connor took over as Program Manager, he made several additional personnel changes including replacing the Engineering Manager. Also, just prior to launch, a new marketing manager was assigned to the project. The net result of all the changes in vision and personnel was a product that had been "neutered," was six months late to market, and priced double the original target. Given its new price of $1,300, the PCjr. was not competitive from a price/performance perspective.

Why did the PCjr. seem to repeat many of the same mistakes made on the DataMaster? One reason was that Don Estrich, who became head of the Entry Systems Division (of which the PCjr. was part), had not been through the trials and tribulations experienced on the DataMaster. He was not on the DataMaster project; he came from the Series 1 and System 7 minicomputer projects. Thus, he did not experience the consequences of senior IBM management changing the DataMaster project in mid-stream, escalating the price, and missing the window of opportunity. The minicomputer market was much less turbulent than the PC market and hence more forgiving to long development times, launch delays, or price increases. As a result, when Estrich assumed overall division responsibility for the PCjr., he did not insist on the kind of modified new product development process that the IBM PC had used—a process that did not allow the broad range of senior IBM executives to make changes to the product as it progressed. He did not appreciate the importance of getting senior

FIGURE 2. New Product Team learning Strategies

	Existing	New
New	Evolutionary Market Innovation New Market Model Strategy	Discontinuous Innovation New Venture Unit Strategy
Existing	Incremental Innovation Cost Reduction Strategy	Evolutionary Technical Innovation Technology Entrepreneur Strategy

Market (vertical axis: New / Existing)

Technology (horizontal axis: Existing / New)

management to buy-in to the vision in the early stages. The net result of all the changes was a product that was late to market and failed to met both customers' as well as management's expectations.

A Roadmap for Team Learning

These examples demonstrate patterns of learning for discontinuous innovations. They show that teams need:

- excellent Within-Team Learning (encompassing having a clear and shared vision that helps the team focus its learning on a well defined learning domain);
- adequate Market Learning, (focusing on competitive technological alternatives): and
- restricted Cross-Team Learning (including limiting communication between teams).

But, how do the learning practices differ for the three other types of innovations in Figure 1? Is one learning strategy appropriate for all products or must team learning strategies be customized for each project? A sound team learning strategy for one product can be detrimental if applied to another. Figure 2 illustrates four different team learning patterns depending on the degree of newness that an innovation represents to the innovating company.

Cost Reduction

The least extreme form of innovation is Incremental Innovation, where the technology already exists within the innovating firm and the product can be sold through existing channels to an existing customer base. This type of innovation requires a cost reduction orientation. In incremental innovation, Within-Team and Cross-Team Learning becomes critical. Teams must build on the knowledge they have gained by producing the product as well as the knowledge of other teams within the organization. They must strive to refine the production process by reducing waste and overhead, streamlining the process, and improving efficiencies. Only adequate Market Learning is needed because project- and company-specific issues (such as production materials, production-personnel skills, manufacturing equipment, and particular suppliers) limit the learning that can be gleaned from competitors.

The Apple Mac team should have been managed as a cost reduction strategy—building on the successes and failures of the Lisa program. But it was set up as a New Venture Unit and severely restricted Cross-Team Learning. The Mac team considered themselves pirates, independent from other teams. This isolation greatly reduced the ability of the Mac team to build on the knowledge gained by the Lisa team. There was an "us versus them" mentality on the Mac. When Lisa was merged into the Mac division, relations between people on both teams were strained. Ken Okin, who was the Lisa hardware manager, described the tense relationship between the two groups:

> A Lisa person in the Mac division was a second-class citizen, so I never really participated [in Mac's development]. I ended up being exiled to the factory. It was the Mac "group" and the Lisa "Bozos."

New Market Model

When the technology already exists within the innovating firm but the product is being sold to new customers, requiring new channels of distribution and pricing strategies, Within-Team Learning and Market Learning become critical. Evolutionary Market Innovation (the upper left quadrant of Figure 1) requires a new market model and a new marketing strategy to compete and win. Cross-Team Learning plays a limited role with this category of innovation because the company must be willing to change its traditional method of marketing. Overly close ties to other teams may impede the team from developing and using the new models needed to compete. To illustrate, the HP125 team was developing a personal computer, but the team had intimate ties with HP's terminal division. Not only did the HP125 team report through the terminal division, but the two teams were co-located in the same building as the terminal business. As a result, when the HP125 was developed, it was a hybrid product—functioning both as a PC and a terminal. Unfortunately, it did not do either very well nor did it do them cost effectively. As a consequence, the HP125 was unsuccessful in the marketplace.

When teams find that a new market model learning pattern is required, new pricing policies and channels of distribution are typically needed. Understandably, companies need to be convinced that their traditional methods will not work, otherwise they will resist implementing any knowledge gained from Market Learning. In such circumstances, the company has two choices: it can either move the project into a division that is currently serving that market (as was the case with the HP Vectra) or it can form a new autonomous team.

When IBM pursued the PC market, Bill Lowe formed a task force to devise a strategy for the IBM PC. Members on the task force were people he "borrowed," primarily from the DataMaster program. One of the first objectives of the task force was to complete an extensive market analyses to learn about the competition and the needs of the marketplace (Market Learning). With the insights gained from the analysis, the task force developed a detailed roadmap detailing where they were going and how to get there (Within-Team Learning). This roadmap/vision was agreed to by all team members and approved by Frank Cary, IBM's CEO. After Cary approved the project, Lowe and his PC team severed virtually all ties with other IBM teams—both functionally and physically. The team moved to a new location in Boca Raton, Florida. Although the team was composed of many of the DataMaster people who were on the PC task force, once the PC project was given the go-ahead, the team isolated itself from others in the company including people who remained on the DataMaster project (severely restricting Cross-Team Learning).

Technology Entrepreneur

The third form of team learning couples new technology with a currently served market (lower right quadrant of Figure 1). Here, effort focuses on becoming a technology entrepreneur. In Evolutionary Technical Innovation, teams must excel at both Market Learning as well as Cross-Team Learning. The HP85, as an equipment controller, illustrates this learning pattern. The HP85 used several engineers as well as the overall Division Manager, Bob Watson, who were all from HP's instrument controller division. Their perspective with controllers assisted in adding several additional features into the HP85 and aided in positioning it as an instrument controller—a market that proved very successful for the product despite its failure as a PC.

New Venture Unit

When a company is trying to develop and commercialize the most extreme form of innovation—discontinuous innovations that combine new technologies with new markets—a New Venture Unit strategy is needed. This entails forming teams composed of people with relevant technical and marketing expertise; severing ties with the main organization; instituting processes that enhance a team's ability to learn within the context of its own team (which includes establishing a clear vision and getting team members as well as senior management to buy into the vision); and completing a thorough external audit to learn about alternative technologies. Caution must be exercised in completing a customer audit. This is because customers can be poor judges of products and concepts that offer features not previously attainable, as is typically the case in discontinuous innovation. For example, years ago in the automobile industry, if one would have asked customers about their preferences, they would not have indicated a dissatisfaction with having to shift gears manually; yet when the automatic transmission was introduced, it was widely accepted.13 Similarly, as Gassee noted, if you had conducted a conventional consumer marketing survey in the late 1970s, it would likely have indicated a dubious market for personal computers. He said, "In truth, no one really needs a computer until the day he gets one. Then he can't live without it."[14]

If a New Venture Unit strategy is the requisite learning strategy for discontinuous innovation, why did both the PCjr. and Lisa fail despite being set up essentially as New Venture Units? The answers lay not in what the two teams did, but rather in what they didn't do. As was the case with both the PCjr. and the Lisa, intra-group chemistries were poor—most likely stemming from a vision that was neither shared nor stable. Furthermore, with both projects, extensive turnover of key team members was pervasive. Moreover, two additional factors emerged as being detrimental to a New Venture Unit team's ability to learn: team size and allocated resources. When establishing an autonomous New Venture Unit management must exercise care to keep the team small and to operate on a restricted budget. A small group of people who think they are underdogs, who are out to change the world, and who feel they have the cards stacked against them can coalesce into a tightly bound team and can accomplish great feats. Additional resources may very well detract from a New Venture Unit's effectiveness. This issue of resources was evident in Tracy Kidder's landmark book *Soul of a New Machine*. When trying to build the Eagle, a new supermini computer, the team had to fight for resources. As team members recalled, "Sometimes even the pencil supply seemed short."[15]

Conclusions

Table 1 summarizes the patterns of learning needed for the four different types of innovations. Evidence suggests these findings may be generalizable to a wider range of companies and industries. For example, when Corning developed optical fibers for use in telecommunications (new technology in a new market), it pursed a New Venture Unit strategy and formed a separate company with Siemens AG (called Siecor Optical Cables, Inc.) to develop and commercialize optical-fiber cable and components. Within one year of the formation of the

TABLE 1. Team Learning Strategies for Each Innovation Environment

	Within-Team Learning	Cross-Team Learning	Market Learning
Incremental Innovation Cost Reduction Strategy	Extensive	Extensive	Moderate
Evolutionary Technical Innovation Technology Entrepreneur Strategy	—*	Extensive	Extensive
Evolutionary Market Innovation New Market Model Strategy	Extensive	Restricted	Extensive
Discontinuous Innovation New Venture Unit Strategy	Extensive	Restricted**	Moderate***

*Not enough data to determine.

**After the team is formed, ties with other teams should be greatly curtailed or completely severed.

***Good technical analysis isneeded, but caution must be exercised with customer analysis and input—for a discontinuous innovation, the customer may notknow they need or want such an exteme innovation.

venture, optical fiber sales had reached $30 million, up from $5 million three years earlier. Similarly, after Searle scientists discovered the sweet taste of aspartame (a new technology for Searle in a new market), the pharmaceutical company—which had little experience with food additives—created a new company called NutraSweet to handle the further refinement and marketing of its artificial sweetener.[16]

When GE decided to compete in computer axial tomography (CT), a market it was currently serving with its line of x-ray equipment and supplies, the company pursued a Technogy Entrepreneur strategy. The team completed an exhaustive external technical assessment (Market Learning). Company engineers pursued an unrefined approach developed independently by researchers at Stanford University and the Varian Corporation. This technology became known as Fan-Beam technology. GE engineers improved the fan-beam technology (through Within-Team Learning), incorporated their improved technological approach in their CT scanners, and surpassed the performance of even the industry pioneer, EMI. With GE's technologically advanced scanner, the company was able to capture 60% of the CT market—up from zero four years earlier.[17]

Our study shows that having a clear vision and having that vision shared and agreed to by others on the team were reoccurring themes for successful innovation. Successful teams were totally committed to the vision of the project and had a crystal-clear understanding of the goals and objectives of the project. This commitment and understanding helped motivate team members to work extremely long hours (100 hours per week were not uncommon) to accomplish the goal.

However, new product teams must tailor their learning patterns to each project. The Mac team had a clear and shared vision. As Rich Page, an Apple

Fellow who worked on the Lisa and Mac, described it, "There was definitely shared vision and it was definitely laser-beam focused." However, the fundamental reason for the Mac's below-expectation performance was that the team used an inappropriate learning strategy.[18] They tried to use a New Venture Unit strategy when they should have used a Cost Reduction strategy—building on the successes and mistakes of the Lisa. Without the proper learning strategy, commitment and understanding of the team's vision and goals are not enough for successful innovation. Teams must understand and execute an appropriate learning strategy. If they do, then learning just may provide the key to unlocking an organization's knowledge capital.

Notes

1. Gary Lynn, Joseph Morone, and Albert Paulson, "Marketing and Discontinuous Innovation: The Probe and Learn Process," *California Management Review*, 38/3 (Spring 1996): 8-37.

2. See Joseph Bower and Clayton Christensen, "Disruptive Technologies: Catching the Wave," *Harvard Business Review*, 73/1 (January/February 1995): 48-49.

3. Because little information exists on new product team learning and because the guiding questions of this study are of who, what, and how variety (within a historical perspective), an exploratory case study approach was used. Exploratory research can assist the researcher in better defining and describing the problem; it can yield a deeper understanding about a problem or question which may then lead to theory development. These theories can then be tested using descriptive or causal techniques. Hence, the goal of this research is theory building, not theory testing. As an exploratory study, the objective is to increase its internal validity; follow-on descriptive studies can be used to extend its external validity. As a consequence, one industry was chosen: personal computers. Within that industry, one product type was investigated: desktop personal computers. IBM, Apple, and Hewlett-Packard were companies chosen because of their similar product types and the time frames of their respective desktop computer introductions (from 1977 to the mid-1990s). Furthermore, these three companies yield an interesting comparison because each had different perspectives at the time: IBM was a mainframe computer manufacturer, HP was a calculator and scientific-instrument manufacturer, and Apple was a personal computer supplier. For each company, both successful as well as unsuccessful products were studied. Because exploratory longitudinal case studies were employed in this investigation, several measures were used to reduce some of its limitations. First, rigor and reliability were enhanced by using triangulation from several data sources. At least three people on each project team, including the project manager when accessible, were interviewed. The information obtained was verified by internal and external secondary information when available. Second, a well-defined questioning protocol was used. And third, inter-project differences were analyzed to reduce the temptation to jump to conclusions based on limited data. The exploratory methodology I used was consistent with that as recommended by K. M. Eisenhardt, "Building Theories from Case Study Research," *Academy of Management Review*, 14/4 (1989): 532-550; and R. K. Yin, *Case Study Research, Design and Methods* (Newbury Park, CA: Sage Publications, 1989).

4. For Apple, interviewees included: Randy Battat, Jim Bean, Bob Belleville, Ed Birss, Mike Boich, Ed Colby, Mike Connor, John Couch, Chris Espinosa, Chuck

Franklin, Martin Haberli, Eric Harslem, Andy Hertzfeld, Wil Houde, Mike Kane, Guy Kawasaki, Dan'l Lewin, Ken Okin, Rich Page, Taylor Pohlman, Jef Raskin, Wayne Rosing, Wendell Sander, Barry Smith, Steve Wozniak, and Barry Yarkoni; for IBM: Dave Bradley, Larry Duffy, Lew Eggebrecht, Bob Ellinghausen, Noel Fallwell, Mel Hallerman, Pat Harrington, Doug LeGrande, Bill Lowe, Jeannette Mahr, Ike Mediate, Ron Mehaffey, David O'Connor, Gary Pitt, Larry Rojas, Joe Sarubbi, Bill Sydnes, Jan Winston, and Jesse Zuckor; and for HP: Jim Bausch, Bob Bowden, Tom Buiocchi, Jim Carlson, Deme Clainos, Jacques Clay, Bruce Foster, Jim Groff, Dick Grote, Dick Hackborn, Larry Kelly, Webb McKinney, Tim Mikkelsen, Carol Mills, Rick Nelson, Alan Nonnenberg, Mike Perkins, John Price, Craig Sanford, Kent Stockwell, Srinivas Sukumar, Dan Terpack, Jim White, and Andrew Zaremba.

5. For a discussion of Boeing, see Hirotaka Takeuchi and Ikujiro Nonaka, "The New New Product Development Game," *Harvard Business Review*, 64/1 (January/February 1986): 137-146. For a more in-depth discussion of Within-Company learning, see George S. Day, "Learning About Markets," *Marketing Science Institute*, Report 91-117, June 1991; K. Imai, I. Nonaka, and H. Takeuchi, "Managing the New Product Development Process," in K. Clark, R. Hayes, and C. Lorenz, eds., *The Uneasy Alliance* (Boston, MA: Harvard Business School Press, 1985), pp. 337-375.

6. Krista McQuade and Benjamin Gomes-Casseres, "Mips Computer Systems," in Robert Burgelman, Modesto Maidique, and Steven Wheelwright, eds., *Strategic Management of Technology and Innovation* (Chicago, IL: Irwin, 1996), pp. 259-274.

7. We tried not to use "failure" to describe the projects that we studied. The term "failure projects" must be used with caution. Although the Mac and Lisa, for example fell far short of their sales forecast they did set the stage for the very successful Mac+.

8. See, for example, H. I. Ansoff, *The New Corporate Strategy* (NY: John Wiley & Sons 1988); Gary Lynn, Aaron Shenhar, and Dov Dvir, "Integrative Product-Project Classifications: Implications for Business Innovation and Cross-Functional Management," International Conference on Management of Technology (IAMOT), Gotenborg, Sweden, 1997; R.T. Moriarty and T.J. Kosnik, "High-Tech Concepts, Continuity, and Change," *IEEE: Engineering Management Review* (March 1990), pp. 25-35.

9. Guy Kawasaki, *Selling the Dream* (New York, NY: HarperCollins, 1991).

10. Peter Nulty, "Apple's Bid to Stay in the Big Time," *Fortune*, February 7, 1983, pp. 36-41.

11. Michael Moritz, *The Little Kingdom* (New York, NY: William Morrow, 1984), p. 320.

12. For more discussion of core rigidity, see Dorothy Leonard-Barton, *Wellsprings of Knowledge* (Boston, MA: Harvard Business School Press, 1995).

13. J. Durgee, "New Product Ideas from Focus Groups," *The Journal of Consumer Marketing*, 4 (Fall 1978) :57-65.

14. J. Gassee, *The Third Apple* (New York, NY: Harcord Brace Jovanovich, Inc., 1987), p. 60.

15. Tracy Kidder, *Soul of a New Machine* (Boston, MA: Little Brown & Company, 1981), p. 225.

16. Gary S. Lynn, "Understanding Products and Markets for Radical Innovation," Ph.D. dissertation, Rensselaer Polytechnic Institute, Troy, NY, 1993.

17. Lynn, Morone, and Paulson, op. cit.

18. The Mac was to be Apple's salvation—to make up for the III and Lisa debacle. The Mac was launched on January 24, 1984. It was a graphical user interface (GUI), mouse-operated computer powered by the Motorola 68000, and came with 128K of RAM, 64K of ROM, a 9" monitor, and a 3.5"-400K floppy—for $2,495. The Mac sold well to individuals, but poorly to its primary target market which was

corporations. In the Mac business plan, sales in the first year were forecasted to reach 425,000 units world-wide and 354,500 in the United States. Unfortunately, total sales only reached 174,000 in 1984 and 245,000 in 1985. It was not until three years later, after Apple launched the Mac+ in 1986, that Mac sales achieved what was forecasted to be sold in the first year.

IDEO PRODUCT DEVELOPMENT

(S. Thomke / #9-600-143 / 21 p)

Summary

This Harvard Business School case study describes IDEO, the world's leading product design firm, and its innovation culture and process. Emphasis is placed on the important role of prototyping and experimentation in general, and on the design of the successful Palm V handheld computer in particular. A studio leader is asked by a business startup (Handspring) to develop a novel handheld computer (Visor) in less than half the time it took to develop the Palm V, requiring several shortcuts to IDEO's legendary innovation process.

Outline

History of IDEO
Design Philosophy and Culture
IDEO's Innovation Process
The Palm V Project
The Handspring Project

Learning Objectives

- Understand the prototyping and experimentation practices of a leading product developer
- Recognize the respective roles of playfulness, discipline, and structure in innovation processes
- Understand the challenges of building and managing a company with an unusually creative and innovative corporate culture

Questions, Ideas, and Exercises

1. Consider the IDEO emphasis on "quick and dirty prototyping" and the possible advantages it brings to product development. Using the IDEO method, claims founder David Kelley, "you could never design a VCR you couldn't program. [Researchers at larger companies] are afraid of looking bad to management, so they do an expensive, sleek prototype, but then they become committed before they really know any of the answers." To what extent is your firm developing quick, rough prototypes of new product ideas? Is your culture prepared to accept, or even to pursue, rapid early failure in the interest of recognizing and solving fundamental design problems faster?

2. Note that Exhibit 3 presents in detail the four-phase IDEO process. If you are anticipating or just beginning the development of a new product, hold a meeting of your product development team to imagine your way through the IDEO phases. Be

as concrete as you can in projecting your product into IDEO's scheme. Pay special attention to cultural and structural challenges that surface during this exercise. Then, working with colleagues who participated, try to characterize in writing the key differences between your firm's approach to product development and IDEO's. Are there important lessons your company can learn from IDEO?

3. If you were running IDEO, would you accept the Handspring project? If so, would you ask Handspring to change its aggressive launch schedule?

IDEO Product Development

"I should have had café latte," thought Dennis Boyle as he was sipping his strong espresso at Peet's coffeehouse, just around the corner from his office. Many designers and engineers from his company, IDEO, one of the world's largest and arguably most successful product development firms, often gathered here and talked. It was late summer 1998 in Palo Alto, the heart of California's Silicon Valley, and Boyle gathered his thoughts for a meeting with David Kelley, the head and founder of IDEO.

Boyle had just led his group at IDEO through the development of 3Com's Palm V hand-held computer, which designers and managers at both firms already considered a successful product with very large commercial potential. Now he was being asked to design the competing Visor product by the very same individuals he had worked with previously. The only twist was that these clients themselves now worked at Handspring, a new venture whose goal was to come out with a fully compatible, slightly smaller and less expensive palm-size computer that could easily add functionality. 3Com had even licensed out operating software to Handspring.

Although working on the Palm V challenged IDEO's engineering skills, working with Handspring promised to challenge the very manner in which it operated. It operated on the principle of getting all team members to "fail often to succeed sooner"—a creative process that often looked to outsiders like "spinning wheels." The process usually generated a fountain of absurd-appearing but innovative ideas before the final answer and product miraculously came through a process of discipline and fast decision-making.

The IDEO philosophy melded Californian iconoclasm with a genuine respect for new ideas and invention. For over two decades, the firm contributed to the design of thousands of new products ranging from the computer mouse to the stand-up toothpaste dispenser. Along the way, it had also become the largest award-winning design firm in the world (see **Exhibit 2**). IDEO came to national prominence when ABC's Nightline illustrated its innovation process by showing its designers re-engineer a decades-old icon, the supermarket shopping cart, in just five days.

Now Boyle had to decide whether he should suggest to Handspring's management to add more time to a development schedule that was less than half of what it took to design the stunningly beautiful and innovative Palm V. Boyle's group feared that an overly aggressive development schedule would require them to bypass many of the early development stages that the firm was particularly good at and, at the end, deliver a product that could be so much better if they just had more time.

Professor Stefan Thomke and Ashok Nimgade, M.D. prepared this case as the basis for class discussion rather than to illustrate either effective or ineffective handling of an administrative situation.

History of IDEO

[David Kelley] and the company he heads, IDEO of Palo Alto, has designed more of the things at our fingertips than practically anyone else in the past 100 years, with the possible exception of Thomas Edison.

—San Francisco Examiner[1]

It was desperation caused by recalcitrant furniture during a college move that drove David Kelley to enter the Carnegie-Mellon campus workshop in search of a saw. The sights and sounds of the strange new world captured the fancy of the electrical engineering major from Ohio. For a while, in fact, he considered switching majors to fine arts but stayed with engineering. The internal switch that flickered on, however, would lead Kelley to leave engineering jobs at Boeing and NCR to embark on the journey that, according to *Fortune* Magazine, would make him "one of the most powerful people in Silicon Valley." But the first thing Kelley would ever actually design of consequence was a telephone that could only ring one number: his own. He presented this to his college girlfriend.

In 1975, Kelley joined the Stanford University program in product design. These were heady days with Kelley finding that "In Silicon Valley everything was new. . . there were no preconceived notions."[2] Through part-time consulting experience, Kelley found to his surprise that most consulting firms consisted of specialists, with technological companies lacking clear access to a general product development firm. In 1978, amid the Silicon Valley boom, Kelley gave up writing his Ph.D. thesis. (Nonetheless, even without a formal Ph.D. he would become a professor at Stanford University.)

Kelley went on to form and run David Kelley Design for the next decade. IDEO started in 1991 when David Kelley Design merged with two companies: ID Two, led by renowned designer Bill Moggridge, and Matrix, started by Mike Nuttall. The name IDEO came to life when Bill Moggridge scanned his dictionary for suitable names and liked "ideo-" (a Greek word which meant "idea") as it formed the foundation of many important combined words such as *ideo*logy and *ideo*gram. Kelley, whose company was larger than the other two combined, took over as chief executive of the new firm.

The merger brought under one umbrella all services client companies needed to design, develop, and manufacture new products: mechanical and electrical engineering, industrial design, ergonomics, information technology, prototype machining, and even cognitive psychology. IDEO thus pioneered the design version of "concurrent engineering"—a fusion of art and engineering to produce aesthetically pleasing products that were also technically competent.[3] As an example of the utility of concurrent engineering, consider how the decision to add air vents to a computer to prevent overheating might detract from the product's streamlined aesthetics if the designers and engineers failed to work together closely.

The hardest places to practice concurrent engineering, quite understandably, were in devices involving compact and complex design such as automotive components, medical instruments, and small computing devices where small changes would have often unforeseeable ripple effects on components far removed. IDEO, with its equal emphasis on design and engineering, took up many of

---

[1] R. Garner, *San Francisco Examiner*, May 23, 1994, p. B-1.

[2] L. Watson, "Palo Alto Product Designer Finds Business Booming," *The San Francisco Chronicle*, August 3, 1992, p. C3.

[3] J. Lew, "Of mice and Miatas: Design shops shape our lives," *San Francisco Examiner*, August 12, 1992, p. 4·

these challenges. In contrast, its leading competitors historically had stressed industrial design over engineering.

Major IDEO clients included Apple Computer, AT&T, Samsung, Philips, Amtrak, Steelcase, Baxter International, and NEC Corp. IDEO's thirst for variety led it to complete thousands of projects, including 50 projects for Apple Computer (including its first mouse), ski goggles, the Avocet Vertech Skiers watch, and a large variety of medical instrumentation. The company also participated in Hollywood film projects, creating scale-model submarines for "The Abyss" and a 25-foot mechanical whale for "Free Willy". In the 1990s, IDEO won more industry awards than any other design firm worldwide (see **Exhibits 2 and 4**).

In the late 1990s, IDEO employed over 300 staff and maintained design centers in Boston, Chicago, San Francisco, London, Palo Alto, Grand Rapids, New York, Milan, Tel Aviv, and Tokyo. The sites were chosen for their stimulating locations. Although all centers operated independently, seeking business locally, they exchanged a high volume of e-mail and often shared talent as needed. Over the years, while his employees focused on designing client products, Kelley increasingly found himself designing and re-designing IDEO. "I'm more interested in the methodology of design . . .," according to Kelley. "I'm the person who builds the stage rather than performs on it."

Part of this stage-building involved studying the IDEO environment in new ways. Instead of merely relying on employee surveys, the company also studied workplace interactions through suspended video cameras in order to optimize office design.[4] IDEO also sought to improve its own design processes by reviewing all completed projects. According to Kelley, "We pick the things each client does well, and assimilate them into our methodology. We're not good at innovating because of our flawless intellects, but because we've done thousands of products, and we've been mindful."[5]

With corporate downsizing of the 1990s, IDEO and other design firms flourished as companies outsourced more design projects. IDEO's fees generally ran from as little as $40,000 to over $1 million, depending on the scope of the project. The privately held company remained tightlipped about revenues, but in 1996 was known to have revenues of $40-$50 million. Revenues came from about 30% each in medical, consumer, and telecommunications/computers with an additional 10% from industrial products.[6]

IDEO came to national prominence when it allowed ABC to televise a segment showing its designers meeting the challenge of re-engineering the commonplace shopping cart—a virtually unchanged icon for the past several decades, despite its creaky and obdurate wheels and often unwieldy basket—in just five days. The IDEO design replaced the traditional large basket with a system of baskets that allowed consumers to use the shopping cart as a "base camp" for shopping. Innovative new wheels allowed greater maneuverability in the store. Hooks on the frame would allow for bagged items to be transported out to the parking lot. The lack of a central basket removed much of the incentive for stealing the shopping carts.

---

[4] P. Roberts, P, "Live! From your office! It's...," Fast Company, October 1999.

[5] T.S. Perry, "Designing a Culture for Creativity," *Research Technology Management*, March 1995, v. 38(2), pp. 14-17.

[6] R. Rosenberg, *The Boston Globe*, "By design, these firms take on other companies' products," May 11, 1997, p. C1.

Design Philosophy and Culture

If a picture is worth a thousand words, a prototype is worth ten thousand.

—IDEO innovation principle

Central to IDEO's design philosophy was the role of prototyping. According to Tom Kelley, general manager and David Kelley's brother, "we prototype more than our clients suspect, and probably more than our competitors." Frequent prototyping served as the most important way for his company to communicate with clients, marketers, experts, and end users. Prototypes ensured everyone was imagining the same design during discussions about a product. All IDEO offices had shops staffed by highly skilled machinists to rapidly produce both simple and sophisticated prototypes. Quite often, according to Whitney Mortimer, a Harvard MBA who joined the firm in the late '90s, "the real 'aha's' in product development occur here."

But in the early stages, perfecting a sophisticated model was considered a waste of time. "You learn just as much from a model that's wrong as you do from one that's right," according to engineer Steve Vassallo. Thus, designers and engineers themselves created early prototypes from readily available material such as cardboard, foamcore, Legos, and Erector sets.

Rapid prototyping at IDEO followed the three "R's": "Rough, Rapid, and Right!" The final R, "Right," referred to building several models focused on getting specific aspects of a product right. For example, to design a telephone receiver, an IDEO team carved dozens of pieces of foam and cradled them between their heads and shoulders to find the best shape for a handset. "You're not trying to build a complete model of the product you're creating," per Vassallo. "You're just focusing on a small section of it."[7]

Quick and dirty prototyping allowed for a greater number of iterations. "By our method," David Kelley claimed, "you could never design a VCR you couldn't program. [Researchers at larger companies] are afraid of looking bad to management, so they do an expensive, sleek prototype, but then they become committed to it before they really know any of the answers. You have to have the guts to create a straw man." At IDEO, these straw men were repeatedly knocked down, a process which left IDEO's staffers with thick skin. "Failure," Kelley felt, "is part of the culture. We call it enlightened trial and error."[8]

In an allied process, IDEO sought to generate as many ideas as possible early in the design process through almost daily brainstorming sessions. A much-used paraphrased quotation from Einstein epitomized the playfulness of the early stage: "If at first an idea does not sound absurd, then there is no hope for it." The entire process resembled a funnel, with several ideas at the top, three or four at the base, and only one making it all the way through. People were generally not upset if their idea did not become the definitive solution since the act of clipping off ideas brought the entire team closer to the solution – similar to legendary baseball batter Babe Ruth who outlined his strategy once as, "Every strike I make gets me closer to a home run." In addition, discarded ideas were archived and sometimes kept for possible future products.

Sometimes in the course of a project, when progress appeared to come to a standstill, the leader could call for what has come to be known as a Deep Dive® approach. In this process, the team

---

[7] T.S. Perry, "Designing a Culture for Creativity." *Research Technology Management*, March 1995, v. 38(2) pp. 14-17.

[8] Ibid.

would focus intensively for an entire day to generate a large number of creative concepts, weed out weak ideas, and start prototyping based on the top handful of solutions.

To an outsider, however, the entire process could appear messy. "The nature of the organization is very much like David Kelley's mind," says Arnold Wasserman who was part of IDEO's innovation strategy group. "Both are seriously playful and messy. And both are comfortable with confusion, incomplete information, paradox, irony, and fun for its own sake."[9]

The inherent inability to precisely predict the innovation process' outcome, time and cost made it extremely important to keep clients involved. At the beginning of a new project, IDEO would submit cost and time estimates to potential clients. As a project unfolded and designers came up with innovative ideas and concepts, project managers had to ensure that those concepts were within agreed upon budgets and timelines. However, designers often aimed for perfection which could potentially lead to cost and time overruns – also known as "creeping elegance" in design circles – and clients needed to be aware of those opportunities for further innovation and the cost and time involved. As a result, IDEO required very frequent client meetings where all those issues would be discussed.

After a visit to the company's Palo Alto office, business writer Tom Peters likened IDEO to a veritable playground. In his words, "IDEO is a zoo. Experts of all flavours co-mingle in offices that look more like cacophonous kindergarten classrooms. . . . Walk into the offices of IDEO design in Palo Alto, California, immediately you'll be caught up in the energy, buzz, creative disarray and sheer lunacy of it all. Breach the reception area at XYZ Corp . . . and you'll think you've walked into the city morgue."[10]

In keeping with its playroom atmosphere, on Mondays all company branches held "show-and-tells" where designers and engineers could showcase their latest insights and products. Also, of increasing importance to designers was IDEO's "Tech Box," the company's giant "shoebox" for curiosities and interesting gadgets meant to inspire innovators. Designers could rummage through the contents and play with the switches, buttons, and odd materials in search of new uses. The Tech Box included some 300 objects ranging from an archery bow based on pulleys to heat pipes that would turn uncomfortably hot almost the moment they were placed in a cup of hot water.

The culture itself reflected the importance that management attached to creating a democracy of ideas. Most design firms had less than two dozen employees. Growing IDEO to 300 employees involved keeping each unit small. Thus, growth was achieved by budding out smaller design studios whenever one appeared to grow too large. Much quoted was David Kelley's confident assertion in 1990 that "This company will never be larger than 40 people."[11] Following an amoeboid growth strategy, even in a small section of Palo Alto, found the company in possession of nine different buildings in the late '90s.

Employees were encouraged to design their own workspace to reflect their own personalities. Some strung up their bicycles on pulleys. Rolling doors could quickly seal offices for privacy. Staffers kept personal possessions in portable bookshelves and cabinets so that moves between projects could be accomplished rapidly. One studio suspended the wing of a DC-3 airplane with a blinking red winglight from the ceiling.

In keeping with Silicon Valley informality, the company discouraged formal titles and did not mandate a dress code. Management encouraged employees to leave their desk and walk around,

---

[9] R. Garner, *San Francisco Examiner*, May 23, 1994, p. B-1.

[10] T. Peters, "The Peters Principles," *Forbes ASAP*, September 13, 1993, p. 180.

[11] B. Katz, "A leadership style," *Persepctive*, Fall 1999.

especially during mental blocks. "It's suspicious when employees are at their desk all day," according to general manager Tom Kelley, "because it makes you wonder how they pretend to work." IDEO paid high rent for its prime Silicon Valley location so as to encourage stimulating interactions between employees. Free, unlocked loaner bicycles at the Palo Alto lobbies also facilitated movement between each building. Designers were encouraged to talk to one another or even call a brainstorming session through email.

Management rarely fired employees. "We do a better job of managing good employees than of weeding out lower performing employees," David Kelley admitted. "But with small studios, there's literally nowhere to hide for noncontributors." High-performing employees were rewarded by being given more challenging projects to lead. Each employee was assessed through peer review sessions, with peers chosen by the employee. Management also sought to reward high performers through more shares in its client venture capital base.

Through much of the 1990s, turnover, at less than 5% per year, was shockingly low by Silicon Valley standards. The company typically recruited young individuals out of its own internship programs. Recruiting was a long process, entailing meeting with 10 staff members, often over lunch. A disproportionate number of recruits came from Stanford University, where Kelley continued to serve as a professor.

An individual could work on one large project as a principal or on as many as three to four projects as a contributor. IDEO was a flat organization to an extreme. All work was organized into project teams, which formed and disbanded for the life of a project. As a result there were no permanent job assignments or job titles. There were no organization charts or titles to distract from the quality of the work. Project leaders often emerged on the basis of personal excitement about a project. Motivation from peer pressure also spurred employees to put in 50- to 60-hour weeks in creative endeavors.[12]

The lack of hierarchy also avoided the problem of promoting designers and engineers into administrative positions and out of their first love: creating products. But the "no-policy policy" could make for confusion among new recruits. Even proponents of the IDEO culture, including veteran Larry Shubert, admitted that "The culture is partly to be comfortable with ambiguity and confusion. . . . We err on the side of autonomy. There's some discomfort, yes."[13]

But growth appeared to bring its own changes. According to Jeff Smith, president of the Palo Alto-based Lunar Design and an admirer of IDEO, "How well they're able to remain creative and not become bureaucratic and politicized will be very interesting. There's rumor of politics and agendas. . . ." Even David Kelley admitted some increase in bureaucratization. "People are talking about it like it's a company. 'Is it o.k. to invite my wife to this?' Nobody ever asked me that before... Or, 'Is it o.k. if I go home and mow the lawn this afternoon?' Of course, it's o.k."[14]

By the late 1990s, however, the turnover had crept up to 10% as the promise of unparalleled high-tech wealth at Internet-based firms beckoned employees. To counter the trend of increasing attrition, IDEO sought to redo its compensation strategy, planning to do more equity deals and seek royalties.

---

[12] T.S. Perry, "Designing a Culture for Creativity." *Research Technology Management*, March 1995, v. 38(2) pp. 14-17.

[13] S. Orenstein, "The doyen of design," Stanford: May/June 1996, pp. 74-79.

[14] Ibid.

IDEO's Innovation Process

It is inconceivable that the head guy in any organization will know all the answers.

—David Kelley, IDEO founder

If prototyping was central to IDEO's design process, brainstorming was central to its methodology. The two processes, actually, went hand in hand, with brainstorming sessions leading to rapid prototyping or vice versa. The goal was to quickly create a whirlwind of activity and ideas, with the most promising ideas developed into prototypes in just days. The firm followed several principles of brainstorming: stay focused on the topic; encourage wild ideas; defer judgment to avoid interrupting the flow of ideas; build on the ideas of others (since it was usually more productive than seeking glory for one's own insights); hold only one conversation at a time to ensure that introverts also got their say; go for quantity (very productive brainstorming could generate 150 ideas in 30 to 45 minutes); and be visual, since sketching ideas would help people understand them.

Throughout a single project, the project leader might hold brainstorming sessions, or "brainstormers." No more than eight invitees attended these sessions, which ran under the above rules. IDEO personnel viewed invitations to these sessions as a sign of worth and rarely turned them down. In an organization whose lobbies sported large bowls of M&M chocolates, David Kelley once said "brainstormers are the candy. . . . You are in the middle of a project, handling endless details, and then you get invited to a brainstormer, where you get to have all sorts of good ideas and leave with no responsibility for them. It's cathartic, to dump your ideas."[15]

IDEO's product development process followed several phases (see **Exhibit 3** for details). In **Phase 0 ("Understand/Observe")**, the team sought to understand the client's business and immersed itself in finding out about the feasibility of a product. This involved inhaling everything ever written about the planned product and potential users. By the end of this process, team members tacked to the project center walls pictures and diagrams summarizing major discoveries about the marketplace and users. In the closely related **Phase I ("Visualize/Realize")**, the team ended up choosing a product direction based on ideas, technologies, and market perceptions. The team also gained an understanding of the product context through a gallery of envisioned characters using the product in their daily lives. By the end of Phase I, through close coordination with the client, the team would have rough three-dimensional models of a product and a general idea of the manufacturing strategy to be utilized.

In **Phase II ("Evaluating/Refining")**, the team enhanced design prototypes through testing functional prototypes. Emphasis shifted over the course of this stage from human factors and ergonomics to engineering. Phase II culminated with a functional model as well as a "looks like" design model. Then in **Phase III ("Implement/Detailed Engineering")**, the team completed product design and verified that the final product worked and could be manufactured. Although engineering efforts predominated, continuous low-level involvement with design team members occurred. By the end of this phase, the team delivered a fully functional design model, tooling databases, and technical documentation. Finally, in **Phase IV ("Implement/Manufacturing Liaison")**, the team ensured smooth product release to manufacturing as the product moved from the shop floor to the client's factory lines.

---

[15] T.S. Perry, "Designing a Culture for Creativity." *Research Technology Management*, March 1995, v. 38(2) pp. 14-17.

But despite the phases delineated above, IDEO had mixed feelings about formalizing any aspect of the innovative process. According to European director Tim Brown, "It's a delicate balance between process and innovation. . . . It's no good if you crank the handle and you know exactly what is going to come out the other end. You also have to be prepared to fail a lot. The great thing about a prototype culture like ours is that we have lots of spectacular failures. We celebrate that."[16]

Nonetheless, armed with the tools of rapid prototyping, brainstorming, and a well-honed product development process, the company viewed itself as being able to provide value to virtually any client. The very diversity and experience of its personnel ensured that it would rarely encounter entirely new problems. Occasionally, however, the company found itself swimming out of familiar water. Once, for instance, the governor of Hawaii asked IDEO about how the state should proceed with its economic reforms.

The Palm V Project

Never go to a client meeting without a prototype.

—"Boyle's Law" (per Dennis Boyle of IDEO; not to be confused with the law of pressure & volume named after 17th century physicist Robert Boyle)

In the mid 1980s, with the advent of Apple Computer's Newton pad, handheld computing got its start and met its near-demise. This revolutionary feature-laden product proved ahead of its time, with consumers frustrated by the sometimes slow and inaccurate handwriting recognition system that was meant to replace the tyranny of the cumbersome keyboard. Users also found the system large and inconvenient. It took until March 1996 before anyone could successfully introduce another general-purpose handheld computing device. This honor belonged to California-based engineer-visionary Jeff Hawkins, whose "Palm Pilot" found almost immediate consumer acceptance. Key to Hawkins' success was the development of critical technologies, including the so-called Graffiti program for handwriting recognition and "syncing," the capability to synchronize data between a handheld computer and a home computer.

Hawkins possessed a maniacal focus on product simplicity. This led him to hone his vision by carrying a crude wood prototype the size of a deck of cards in his pocket while envisioning how typical customers might use the product through the course of a day. Sometimes he would sit through staff meetings scrawling imaginary notes onto the inert wood screen of the prototype. The end result proved a product meant to compete with paper rather than with larger computers. Although it could just store addresses, telephone numbers, a calendar, and a to-do list, it did so rapidly and conveniently.

For all its apparent simplicity, the Palm Pilot became the fastest-selling computer product ever.[17] Hawkins and his staff achieved their feat of design and engineering while working during a period of corporate upheaval that saw their parent company change from Palm Company to U.S. Robotics to 3Com. Understandably, the Palm Pilot success story attracted other start-ups and entrants to the new field, leading to handheld devices touting features such as vibrating alarms, voice recording, increased memory, and so on. One advertisement for the competing Everex Freestyle palm-sized computer, after listing several new features, warned: "Palm Pilot beware!"[18] Microsoft

---

[16] D. Dearlove, "Innovation from the chaos," *The Times* (U.K.), August 13, 1998.

[17] P.E. Teague, "Special Achievement Award: Jeff Hawkins," *Design News*, March 6, 2000, p. 108.

[18] D. Roth, "Putting fluff over function," *Fortune*, March 15, 1999.

itself was expected to enter the field with a new product that would leapfrog current products by offering eight megabytes of memory.

At the Palm division, while many engineers pondered new ways to retain market share, Hawkins recalled thinking, "Who cares. I don't need eight megabytes; I can't even fill up two. Let's show the world that this isn't about speeds and feeds. . . . It's about simplicity."[19] To avoid being caught up in the battle over new features and minutiae, the Palm division under Hawkins' leadership sought an entirely new approach, one that would also hopefully draw in more female users into a market of predominantly male businessmen.

Palm eventually turned to IDEO to fulfill Hawkins' vision. Within IDEO, the choice of project leader fell naturally to Dennis Boyle, a senior project leader and studio manager who had left his mark on the company with a stream of successful products and the institution of the Tech Box, a natural outgrowth of his tendencies since childhood (to the chagrin of this mother) to collect curios of all sorts in shoeboxes. For Boyle, the fit was natural: the very moment he first saw the Palm Pilot he knew "this will make a big difference" and proceeded to use it, add it to his collection, and discuss it at staff meetings. Palm was to remain Boyle's main client for the duration of the project, with a majority of his billable time dedicated there.

For Hawkins' and Boyle's teams, inspiration came from the sleek Motorola StarTac mobile phone that was introduced in 1996 at the price of $1,000— at a time when many mobile phone makers started giving away their products in return for user subscription fees. Hawkins recalled that, "The StarTac was a radical departure. It looked different, beautiful. It also commanded outrageous prices. We wanted to do the same thing."[20] Other products that inspired the IDEO team, and which Boyle kept in his briefcase, included a metal Canon minicamera, Pentax opera glasses, and a telescoping pair of eyeglasses in a thin metal case used as emergency back-up eyewear.

Each of these small and elegant products made the existing line of Palm Pilots appear stodgy in comparison. This was not surprising given that the computer world had generally ignored design in favor of technical bells and whistles that catered to men. Men, after all, comprised the majority of computational gadget users at the time. This mindset was successfully challenged by Apple Computer, which true to its "Think Different" advertisement campaigns, came up with its translucent turquoise iMac computers. Apple President Steve Jobs declared, "for most consumers, color is more important than megahertz."

With similar thoughts in mind, Boyle's team outlined plans for a slimmer, sleeker version of the existing Palm Pilot. This called for reducing the thickness from the current 19mm to 11mm and the weight by one-third. According to Janice Robert, the 3Com vice president in charge of the Palm division at the time of the Palm V release: "We want to appeal to people not just on the rational level but the emotional level."[21]

The team started work on what would become the Palm V project late in 1996.[22] At the outset of the "Understand Phase" (**Phase 0**), which lasted 10-12 weeks, the IDEO team realized that despite the popularity of the Palm III, little data existed on user preferences. Boyle therefore started creating his own observational database by purchasing dozens of the Palm Pilots and giving them to colleagues, business friends, spouses, physicians, and representatives from other walks of life.

---

[19] Ibid.

[20] Ibid.

[21] Ibid.

[22] Many viewed the parallels in nomenclature between the Palm III, V, and VII and the BMW 3, 5, and 7 series as 3Com's tribute to BMW's internationally heralded automotive product line.

The rapidly developing obsession of Boyle's team with Palms spread throughout the company: over 200 IDEO staff members throughout the company eventually started using Palms. Feedback through e-mail or through casual hallway conversations quickly started reaching Boyle's team. The team thus became aware of problems concerning the product's susceptibility to breaking after being dropped, rigidity of the case, placement of the battery and memory doors, and location of the stylus holder.

In March 1997, **Phase I** (visualize and realize) started. At the outset, only three to four IDEO designers and engineers were involved. At the project's height of activity, as many as a dozen staffers would become involved. The diverse team included nationalities ranging from as far afield as Taiwan, the Netherlands, and Israel. Boyle deliberately tapped the talent of two female design engineers including senior designer, Amy Han, in hopes of achieving insights that would attract more female users into a marketplace where 95% of the existing Palm users were men.

Han and her colleague Trae Niest, in turn, obtained feedback from 15 other female colleagues. As a group, they challenged the conventional wisdom that handheld devices, in general, had to be square with block edges and colored a mundane gray. Even the advertisements promoted a corporate monolithic blandness, with, for instance, depictions of businessmen slipping Palms into gray suit pockets. The findings and insights of Han and her group led the industrial designers to make the new product more curvy, with tapering edges. The new project bore the code name "Razor," which indicated the goal of Hawkins' team at Palm to create a "razor thin" product.

The IDEO team met weekly with the Palm division to ensure a constant stream of feedback. Boyle made sure the team never went to a client meeting without a prototype of some type or another. The prototypes varied from being as simple as a keypad button to mockups of subtly different-sized LCD panels to styluses of varying thicknesses, lengths, and contours (see **Exhibits 5 and 6**). This process helped ensure that even the smallest of details would be considered. As a result, for instance, the team designed both sides of the device to accommodate a wide variety of potential add-on covers and styluses. Even left-handed individuals would find the dual rail system accommodating.

To ensure a very thin product, the design teams realized early in the process that traditional batteries would have to give way to thinner rechargeable lithium ion batteries. However, it was not clear, considering recharging times and use patterns, that lithium ion would work in this design. The Palm team under Frank Canova, director of hardware engineering, and IDEO spent much of the first half of 1997 corralling reluctant battery makers to cooperate in this venture. Another sticky issue confronting the entire team concerned the use of anodized aluminum for creating the thin casing – a choice of material based on the limitations of plastics – given that US manufacturers had little experience working with this material. As a result, the Palm V team faced the dual challenge of communicating with Asian manufacturers while simultaneously using anodized aluminum to create the technically difficult thin complex surfaces.[23]

By May 1997, conceptualization and realization of the Palm V project gave way to **Phase II** (evaluation and refinement). This stage involved computer-aided design (CAD) engineering to help create accurate industrial models resembling the proposed end product. In this phase, designers and engineers incorporated observed usage patterns to allow users to recharge the Palm for only brief periods of time without shortening battery lives. The team moved toward a final model, choosing solutions, vendors, and sources. Every part of the mechanical model was machined out as close as possible to the final mass-produced parts. By the end of Phase II, some 20-25 prototypes had been created (see **Exhibit 6**).

---

[23] D. Roth, "Putting fluff over function," *Fortune*, March 15, 1999.

In the fall of 1997, **Phase III**, implementation (detailed engineering), started. Every component was engineered to be functional in terms of the electronics and software. Some three to five production prototypes were created. A number of each of these prototypes were built for drop testing to develop the sturdiest possible electronics. Testing was also undertaken to meet government regulations. By the end of Phase III, prototype models could exceed $30,000 each. The team kept refining those models until just one or two final contestants remained. At the same time, the Palm team grew by leaps and bounds, particularly in the realm of production as well as product promotion. Through regular meetings of increasing sizes, and through a flurry of e-mail exchanges, responsibilities gradually shifted away from IDEO.

One of the most bothersome problems confronting the team involved binding the complex 11 mm-wide unit together without a single screw (screws being considered aesthetically and mechanically undesirable by the IDEO designers). The team ultimately committed to using a binding device never before used for handheld computers: industrial glue. At a most inopportune time, however, 3Com's modem card gluers—the only available personnel with experience in using industrial glue—left the company. The remaining team ended up experimenting through trial and error with several different adhesives and bonding parameters before arriving at a satisfactory solution (see **Exhibit 6**).

By end of **Phase IV**, implementation (manufacturing liaison) and expected late fall 1998, "Razor" would be released to production. The Palm division planned to retain some IDEO personnel for another six months—the amount of time projected for gearing up for market release in February 1999. During this period, pilot production would work on smoothing processes at the production line to ultimately allow for manufacturing up to 5,000 units a day. This was crucial: each day's loss of a production line's output would cost the company a few hundred thousand dollars. Many problems still remained for the Palm manufacturers to address including cracks in the display, electrostatic charge, docking problems, cover imperfections, supplies procurement, and component switching. An aggressive schedule would compound problems that would otherwise be considered routine for products of this complexity. Hundreds of personnel were expected to become involved at the manufacturing sites in Utah, Japan, and Singapore as well as at dozens of vendor sites in Hong Kong, Taiwan, California, Texas, and Singapore.

The Handspring Project

In July 1998, both Hawkins and his business partner Donna Dubinsky, a Harvard MBA who had run the business side of Palm, resigned from 3Com on amicable terms to set up shop in Palo Alto. Part of the reason for the move was the desire for greater autonomy. Despite the success of the Palm line, 3Com as a whole was not doing well enough to reward personnel with stock. The goal of the new company was to come out with a fully compatible, slightly smaller, and less expensive clone of the palm-size computers. A technical motivation behind the new company was to address the Palm's inability to easily add functionality.

Hawkins had already scaled back to part-time work at Palm Computing to turn his attention to a long-time interest of his: writing a book on how the brain works. The temptation to interrupt the academic project to take another pass at building the perfect palm-size device was irresistible for someone universally hailed as the "father of a new industry." In quick order, Hawkins and Dubinsky were joined by the original Palm team of a dozen engineers. People enjoyed working with Hawkins, who, in Boyle's words was "by and large an even-keeled, predictable, normal person despite being a brilliant innovator."

Just a few weeks after starting up, Dubinsky and Hawkins, now chief product officer at Handspring, signed a licensing agreement with 3Com for the right to use the Palm operating system.

This agreement would provide any product they developed compatibility with the myriad applications already available for Palm devices. Once again, Hawkins would turn to IDEO for designing a new product.

In July 1998, Hawkins asked Boyle for a proposal. Hawkins felt that the proposed device should be able to easily link-up through so-called "ROM cards" for games, pagers, cell phones, Global Positioning System receivers, voice recorders (the product would have a tiny built-in microphone), wireless modems, MP3 music players, graphing calculators, digital cameras, and even cardiac monitors. A solution for how to do this came to Hawkins when he spotted his child's Nintendo Game Boy, which allowed for changing games simply by inserting interchangeable game cartridges. This led to the so-called "Springboard" slot on the back of the product, which would allow the user to plug in a variety of matchbook-size modules. Hawkins' ten-year-old daughter actually proposed the product name "Visor"—short for "advisor."

The IDEO-Handspring team wanted the modules to be simple to use, with the device operating the moment a module was inserted. Some two dozen third-party developers expressed interest in developing add-on devices for the proposed Visor. Even without a concrete plan, funding flowed easily from venture capitalists eager to duplicate Palm's success with a device that could set a new trend in handheld computing. Publicity, too, would come easily, even in a field replete with new handheld devices. For the meantime, however, the media was kept guessing.

Apart from product features such as price, memory and colors, the Visor team saw little need for market research. According to Dubinsky, "We felt we understood the marketplace pretty well. After all, we invented the product and the category... You can't test the concept of a slot; it's too major."[24] The new project, however, was launched at a time when skeptics noted that people used hand-held devices primarily for mundane tasks such as storing addresses and personal calendars, rather than for complex tasks such as accessing e-mail. "People don't want a combination device," according to Ken Dulaney, mobile computing market research specialist at the Gartner Group. "Every time you try to get a computer to do many things, it ends up doing none of them well."[25]

Hawkins and Dubinsky insisted that the Visor's cost be kept to $150 - a price far below the $300 commanded by the original Palm Pilot in 1996 and the $450 commanded by the Palm V at its market launch. This price was intended to attract a wider following and consistent with Handspring's strategy of getting a product with the new standard into many hands as quickly as possible. As a result, Hawkins and Dubinsky pushed for a product launch deadline of late 1999, just in time for the holiday gift-giving season and several months less than their already ambitious prior deadline of spring 2000. This would entail a product development cycle of about 10 months before handing off the product to production in March-April 1999.

Boyle was not worried about meeting this challenging deadline because IDEO could meet difficult deadlines, even if at the eleventh hour and fifty-ninth minute. Furthermore, the team under Boyle had already encountered and worked smoothly with most of the Handspring team through dozens of prior meetings and other encounters during the Palm V project. IDEO and Handspring shared in common a belief in quick prototyping and a consumer-centered mentality. In Hawkins' words, after all, "I'm not down on engineering, but I'm really down on technology for technology's sake. . . . I don't say 'Put the biggest, meanest CPU in here.' I say, 'Make this work well for the consumer.'"[26]

---

[24] K. Hafner, "One More Ultimate Gadget," *The New York Times*, September 16, 1999, Late Edition, p. G1.

[25] Ibid.

[26] R. Merritt, "Palm Pilot designer steers fresh course in handhelds." *Electronic Engineering Times*, October 25, 1999.

The Handspring project would also require Boyle's team to keep the rest of IDEO, not to mention the rest of Silicon Valley, in the dark about the project. This would make for uncomfortable moments, especially during informal hallway conversations with colleagues, some of whom were still working on the Palm V project.

What concerned Boyle much more, however, was having to sacrifice the IDEO emphasis on innovation and design in order to meet the client's goal. Because of the time and price pressures, Hawkins' proposal would imply running with only "tried-and-true" technology; IDEO would not be able to indulge in the early phases of its legendary development process that differentiated it from other product development firms. Visor would have to sacrifice style and settle on an inexpensive plastic housing, and on AAA batteries instead of the rechargeable lithium-ion battery found in the Palm V.

If they have twice the time, Boyle was confident that his team could help create a killer product that would match the Palm V in design excellence and capability. Should he and Kelley try to persuade Handspring to postpone the Visor launch which would allow the team to follow all the steps of IDEO's legendary innovation process? Or should they just accept the client's request for a very aggressive schedule that would not allow his team to fully engage in early experimentation? He wrestled with these thoughts as he finished his espresso and walked back to the studio to meet David Kelley.

Exhibit 1   Important Milestones

ca. 500 B.C.		Documentation of Egyptian papyrus prototypes for paper, which millennia later remains medium of choice for personal data storage.
1978		David Kelley receives master's degree from Stanford's product design program. Eventually starts up his own company, David Kelley Design.
Mid-1980's		With the advent of Apple Computer's Newton, handheld computing gets its start and meets its near-demise.
1991		IDEO started through a merger between David Kelley Design, ID Two, and Matrix.
1996		Annual IDEO revenues reach $40-50 million.
	March	Engineer-visionary Jeff Hawkins' handheld "Palm Pilot," meant to replace papyrus derivatives rather than computers, finds immediate consumer acceptance.
	Fall	IDEO starts work on the Palm V project, which bears the code name "Razor."
1997	March	Phase I ("Understand") starts on the Palm V project; by May Phase II ("Evaluation and refinement") starts; by fall, Phase III ("Implementation") starts.
1998	Summer	Handspring project starts at IDEO when Jeff Hawkins asks Dennis Boyle for a proposal for proposed handheld computing device with revolutionary "Springboard" slot.
	Fall	Phase IV ends; "Razor" will be released to production. Gearing up for market release starts.
1999	February	First Palm V shipments expected.
	October	Shipment of Handspring Visor planned by Hawkins and Dubinsky, in time for Christmas shopping season.

Exhibit 2   Leading Design Firms and Corporations with Industrial Design Excellence Awards

Design Firms	1995-1998 Awards
IDEO	32
ZIBA Design	20
Fitch	18
Frogdesign	12
Altitude	11
Pentagram	10
Design Continuum	10
Lunar Design	9
Herbst Lazar Bell	7
Hauser	6
Ralph Applebaum Associates	6

Corporations	1995-1998 Awards
Apple	9
Black & Decker	13
Compaq	9
Samsung Electronics	7
Hewlett Packard	5
NCR	9
IBM	5
Microsoft	7
Philips Electronics	6
Thomson Consumer Electronics	7

Source: Business Week's 1999 Design Awards, Industrial Designers Society of America

Exhibit 3   IDEO's Product Development Process Phases

PHASE 0: Understand/Observe

This phase helps the team determine feasibility of designing a product. It involves understanding everything about a new client and its business. Thus, to design a new home entertainment remote control, for instance, the team might study the history of remote controls and the companies involved in designing them. It would research everything from the cost structure of remote controls to the associated panic incidence of "where is the remote control?" syndrome. The team would buy every different kind of remote controls on the market to take apart in a fashion more gentle and controlled than exhibited by frustrated owners.

In addition to meeting with representatives from marketing and manufacturing, the team might also observe people at home on their couches attempting to use remotes. On the topic of consumer observations, IDEO head David Kelley once noted: "That's where most of the good ideas for a new project come."[27] Although this phase was typically the least expensive part of an entire project, product developers at most companies spent little time here for fear of duplicating efforts of marketing or R&D. By the end of Phase 0, the team created a feasibility record along with major discoveries about the marketplace and users.

PHASE I: Visualize/Realize

In the "Visualize/Realize" phase, the product development team visualized potential solutions through tangible prototypes to the point where a product direction was chosen. Although it involved similar activities as Phase 0 (in fact, Phases 0 and I were often combined), it was more product-focused. This intensive stage required close coordination of efforts with the client to ensure constant feedback. By the end of Phase I, the team aimed for having rough three-dimensional models of a product, an understanding of the context in which the product would be used, and an outline of a manufacturing strategy.

The team combined ideas, technologies, and market perceptions with observations of real world users to investigate potential needs that the product could fill. To do this, IDEO eschewed the traditional reliance on statistical data collected by the marketing team in favor of storyboard depictions of lives of several potential users. Use of these fictional characters concretized the product development process. For instance, while designing a better remote system, the IDEO team might conjure up characters like "Jughead the constantly eating couch potato" or "Archie the swinging bachelor" or "Moose the klutz," or "Veronica the princess." Observations of Jughead or Veronica might lead to thoughts about how to avoid spillage of food or nail polish into the buttons; observations of Moose might lead to ideas about developing drop-proof remotes; observations of either Archie or Veronica on a weekend night might lead to design of a remote with large "glow-in-the-dark" buttons that could be hastily be programmed with just one hand in a darkened room.

PHASE II: Evaluating/Refining

The purpose of this stage was to develop functional prototypes and resolve technical problems as well as problems users faced. The emphasis shifted over the course of this stage from human factors and ergonomics to engineering. Concurrent engineering often occurred, through filling in previously unspecified features using an iterative process. This process, of course, required

---

[27] Garner, R., *San Francisco Examiner*, May 23, 1994, p. B-1.

constant communications between various subgroups to ensure that the final outcomes would mesh well together.

By the end of Phase II, a functional model as well as a "looks like" design model was delivered. The industrial design solutions eventually became documented using CAD tools. With finalization of technical specifications, detailed engineering could occur.

PHASE III: Implement (detailed engineering)

During this phase, the team completed product design and verified that the product worked. It validated the manufacturability and performance of the final product. Although engineering efforts predominated, continuous low-level involvement with design team members occurred. For designers, frequent visits to the machine shops during this phase provided a reality check. By the end of this phase, the team delivered a fully functional design model, tooling databases, and technical documentation. Testing might also be undertaken in this phase to meet government regulations. The team also started selecting vendors.

PHASE IV: Implement (manufacturing liaison)

In this phase, the team resolved issues involving the final design to ensure smooth product release to manufacturing as the product moved from the shop floor to the client's factory lines. The team still supervised production of tooling, regulatory approvals, and construction of pilot runs of the manufacturing line. Testing of manufacturing feasibility was crucial: each day's loss of a production line's output might cost the client company a substantial amount in lost revenues. By the end of this phase, the product would be formally handed over to the client.

Source: IDEO

Exhibit 4 Sample of Products Developed by IDEO (See www.ideo.com For More Products)

Product: Apple Mouse
Year: 1983
Client: Apple Computers
Function: Input device for the Apple Lisa and MacIntosh computers

Product: Vertech Alpine/Ski
Year: 1994
Client: Avocet
Function: Sports wristwatch with altimeter; records total feet of ascent or descent per session

Product: Oral-B Squish Grips
Year: 1996
Client: Oral-B
Function: Soft-handled kids' toothbrushes

Product: Heartstream ForeRunner
Year: 1996
Client: Heartstream (now Agilent)
Function: Portable defibrillator for cardiac arrests

Source: IDEO

Exhibit 5 From Concept to Production: Prototyping and Experimentation During the Palm V Project

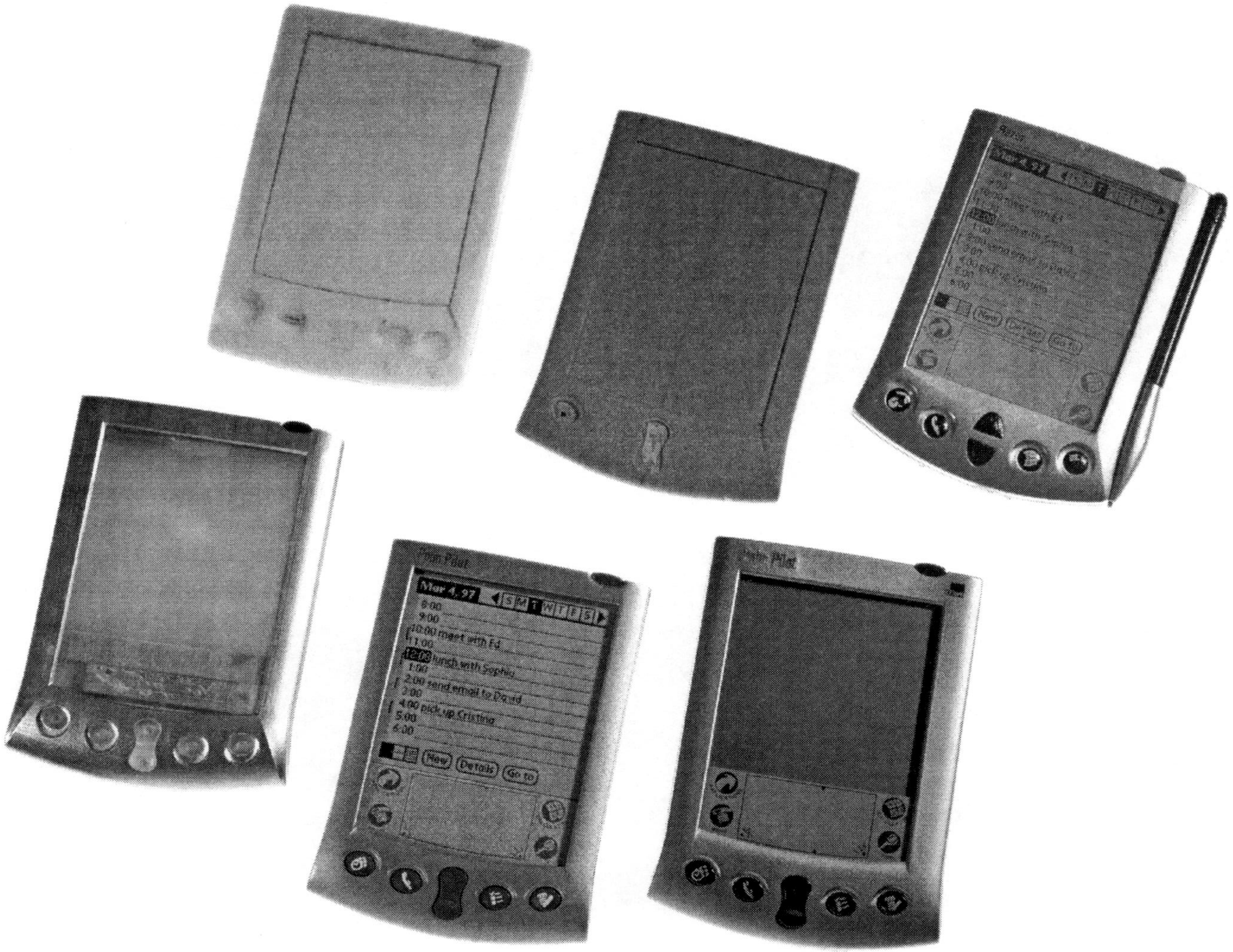

Left to right:

- Low-density foam study
- High-density foam study
- Phase I industrial design prototype with stylus concept

Left to right:

- Machined engineering prototype
- Final industrial design prototype
- Preproduction prototype

Source: IDEO.

Exhibit 6   "Enlightened Trial and Error" at IDEO: Families of Palm V Prototypes

Preliminary Modem Concept Prototypes

Early Industrial Design Form Studies

Prototypes Used for Button Location and Feel Experiments

Foam, Wood and Mechanical Prototypes of HotSync Cradle

Source: IDEO

Exhibit 6 Cont'd   "Enlightened Trial and Error" at IDEO: Families of Palm V Prototypes

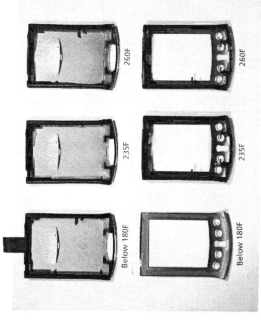

Cover and Stylus Attachment Concept Prototypes

Experimentation to Determine Optimum Glue Bonding Temperatures

Stylus Retention and "Experiential" Mechanical Prototypes

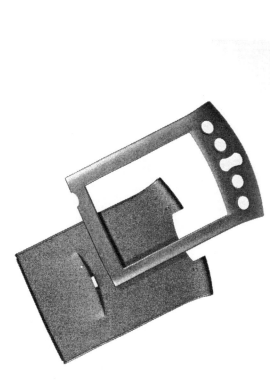

First Articles from Production Case Stampings

Source: IDEO

PRODUCT REJUVENATION:
A LESS RISKY ALTERNATIVE TO PRODUCT INNOVATION

(C. Berenson & I. Mohr-Jackson / #BH019 / 8 p)

Summary

In today's competitive environment, companies that fail to develop new products run a great risk. But new product development poses its own risk: the new-product failure rate is 40 percent for consumer products. A less risky strategy is product rejuvenation: reintroducing an abandoned product or reviving a seriously declining one. Rejuvenation strategies are less costly and take less time. Cost savings are realized in promotions (because of product familiarity), development, channel cooperation, and production and technology. The article notes numerous examples of successful rejuvenation strategies.

Outline

The Advantages of Product Rejuvenation
Approaches to Rejuvenation
Five Steps to Rejuvenation

Learning Objectives

- Understand the opportunities that can arise from reviving old or declining products, and the financial advantages over the development of new products
- Become familiar with key issues to examine and explore in considering a rejuvenation opportunity

Questions, Ideas, and Exercises

1. Apply the authors' "five steps to rejuvenation" to one of your company's declining or abandoned products. If you perceive an opportunity, map out in detail where you think the new value lies and how exactly it might be extracted.

2. Company culture is a significant factor in determining whether your firm would seriously entertain a rejuvenating strategy. Take steps to evaluate your corporate culture on this point. Armed with the strategy plan noted in item 1 above, sound out a few trusted colleagues. Whether they give positive or negative responses, what aspects are they focusing on as they react to your idea? Growth orientation? ("You can't increase revenues 15% yearly by reviving dormant products.") Image? ("Our competitors and customers would think we've run out of new product ideas.") Other factors? If you remain interested in taking your idea to senior management, start to build an information-gathering and communication strategy that deals directly with your colleagues' objections.

151

3. If you are pondering the revival of an abandoned product, take special care not to assume that the product was dropped for sound business reasons. Note the authors' point that "abandonment often occurs because the originator lacks the funds to continue nurturing the product, or feels [perhaps wrongly] that he has better opportunities elsewhere" Consider especially the dramatic example of Cabbage Patch dolls.

Product Rejuvenation: A Less Risky Alternative to Product Innovation

Conrad Berenson and Iris Mohr-Jackson

In today's competitive environment, companies that fail to develop new products are exposing themselves to great risk. Existing products are vulnerable to changing consumer needs and tastes, new technologies, shortening life cycles, and increased domestic and foreign competition.

But companies that develop new products are not without risk either. Out of every 100 products that are marketed, 30 to 35 percent of them fail. Moreover, the new product failure rate is 40 percent for consumer products, 20 percent for industrial products, and 18 percent for services. The failure rate for consumer products is especially high.

Companies lose millions of dollars on their ill-fated products. Texas Instruments lost $600 million in the home computer business; RCA lost $575 million on its videodisc players; Ford lost $350 million on its Edsel; Du Pont lost approximately $100 million on its synthetic leather called Corfam; and the French Concorde aircraft will never recover its losses. When counted in 1994 dollars, these losses would be even greater still.

It is risky to innovate and risky not to innovate. "Product rejuvenation" is one product posture that is less risky than others. Product rejuvenation strategies are twofold. First, they are designed to reintroduce abandoned products. Examples of such products brought back to life are Ipana toothpaste, Black Jack gum, Brylcreem, Fresca, and some Lorimar movies. Second, product rejuvenation strategies are designed to revive seriously declining products. Consider Barbasol shaving cream, Chase and Sanborn coffee, pianos, and Raisinets. By rejuvenating products, companies regain lost market share and generate more profit.

Interest in abandoned or declining products is rising because old brand names already carry value that is becoming increasingly more expensive and risky to create anew. Edward Gustafson, president of the consumer health division of Miles Laboratories— which still produces Miles Nervine, a sedative first introduced in 1882—explains the value of old brand names: "A name is a name is a name, but the reason brands survive is that you have developed an emotional bond between the trademark and the customer" (Saporito 1986). The recent interest in "brand equity" demonstrates increased awareness of the value of old brands.

> *Don't forget those old, "out-of-date" products when considering new market moves.*

THE ADVANTAGES OF PRODUCT REJUVENATION

Most companies fail to realize the potential for rejuvenation. Instead, they turn to new products that appear more promising. However, rejuvenation strategies can offer several significant advantages over new product development.

Less Risk

Rejuvenation strategies are safer than product development, where the odds for success are low. Product development involves risk because of capital shortages, short product life cycles,

Business Horizons
Copyright © 1994
by Indiana University
Kelley School of
Business. For reprints,
call HBS Publishing
at (800) 545-7685.

keen competition, and many other potential pitfalls. To companies with lower risk propensities, the cost involved in rejuvenation is apparently more attractive than the uncertainty inherent in entering new, unfamiliar, and possibly highly competitive growth markets.

Lower Costs

Rejuvenation strategies reduce various types of costs. Promotional costs are reduced because of prior customer familiarity. Product development costs become nonexistent, or nearly so. Fewer expenditures are required to obtain the cooperation of trade channel members. Production and technology costs are cut by capitalizing on past experience with suppliers of equipment, raw materials, and component parts. Prior marketing and distribution experience minimizes time, which translates into lower costs. New products are created from old products at a fraction of the cost incurred in developing new ones from scratch.

Less Time

Rejuvenation strategies also cut time in many ways. Up front product development is not required. Few product alterations are necessary to reintroduce the product. Time is further compressed because companies capitalize on prior manufacturing know-how and on past experience with marketers, distributors, and suppliers of equipment, raw materials, and component parts. Less time translates into lower costs and higher profitability, which in turn enables firms to invest elsewhere.

Cheaper Market Share

Rejuvenating a product is a cheaper way to gain market share than marketing new products that must crash consumers' recognition barriers. For abandoned or declining products, markets exist that are waiting to be served. Compared to new products, for which heavy advertising is needed to build awareness, abandoned and declining products require little or no advertising because of customer familiarity. They can be priced lower because of cost savings in advertising, channel maintenance, and product development, and can yield higher than average returns.

Higher Profits

Abandoned and declining products may be very profitable when handled correctly. Low-growth, small-share businesses (or products) seem to generate more funds than typical startups. They follow narrow product lines, avoid price competition with leaders, and stress product quality. Efficiency, brand recognition, superior product quality, and a precise focus translate into high performance. Rejuvenated businesses can focus their endeavors in many ways—customer type, geography, product characteristics, and so on.

APPROACHES TO REJUVENATION

When a company is trying to breathe new life into older products, two options are available:

1. Reintroducing an abandoned product by marketing it to old or new users.

2. Reviving a seriously declining product by creating new value, then marketing it to old or new users.

Reintroducing Abandoned Products

Abandoned products can be profitable for the firms that reintroduce them, yielding higher than average returns. Reviving old products creates value at minimal costs. Among the cost reductions are:

1. Promotional costs, because of product familiarity;

2. Product development costs;

3. Channel cooperation and relationship costs;

4. Production and technology costs, by capitalizing on past experience with suppliers or equipment, raw materials, and component parts.

Many of the hassles and risks companies experience in developing new products are also eliminated.

Rejuvenation is possible by looking for potential market segments that have special needs, or for customers who crave the old product. An abandoned product may be reintroduced as is to previous users, for whom product adjustments may or may not be necessary. Or it can be reintroduced to a new market where changes are less likely to be necessary.

Old users. Reintroducing an abandoned product to old users requires few, if any, alterations in the product. In some situations, hardcore loyalty may remain strong enough that the product can be marketed at a greatly reduced level of promotion and at the same price or even higher—either of which means good profits.

Product reintroduction is especially feasible when the product has nostalgic value. Abandoned products appeal to consumers who yearn for the brand. Perhaps they evoke pleasant memories of the "good old days," providing vicarious enjoyment of an earlier decade.

A good example of this can be found with the Ebinger bakery name in the New York metropolitan area. Started in 1898, Ebinger's bakery

grew into a chain of 54 stores. The 200 pastries it sold were so extraordinary that a cult-like following developed; it was not unusual for friends and relatives to send monthly packages of Ebinger's goodies to those who had moved out of the area. Customers often stood in line for an hour waiting for delivery from the chain's central bakery to its retail outlets. By 1972, however, the stores had closed. The firm had failed to follow its customers to the suburbs, expanded with poor timing, and fell victim to high-quality mass produced pastries sold at lower prices in supermarkets by such firms as Entenmann's (a General Foods division).

Then the Ebinger brand name (which was in the public domain) was revived by one baker in 1982 and limped along on memories until 1989, when another and better financed baker reintroduced it successfully. The recipes and distinctive packaging have been copied with what appears to be considerable success. Consumers who remembered the "old Ebinger's" are once again putting the distinctive Ebinger's box in their shopping carts.

For many, Beemans, Clover, and Black Jack gums bring back thoughts of childhood years. American Chicle stopped making the sugar-based Black Jack and Clover gums during the 1970s, when the demand for sugarless gum raged. The three were considered "mature brands" with lagging sales, and American Chicle wanted to shift resources to sugarless gums. A decade later, however, Beemans, Clover, and Black Jack were successfully resurrected with the same ingredients, flavoring, and packaging design they had in the 1970s. Their recent success is attributed to their distinctive flavors as well as the nostalgia felt by many who recalled the flavors from childhood.

An old brand name is often remembered many years after abandonment. Not surprisingly, companies have begun attaching a grand old name to a new product to gain market share. Consider the original Packard Bell Company, which made radios in the 1920s and televisions in the 1950s. Like other American consumer electronics firms, the company was in decline by the mid-1970s. The right to use the name of Packard Bell was purchased from Teledyne for less than $100,000 late in 1985. Packard Bell had a rich history and a good name for quality products. Toward the end of 1986, the "new" Packard Bell sold its first products backed by the nostalgic marketing theme, "America grew up listening to us. It still does." Merchandising know-how, good products, and the grand old name sufficed to win Packard Bell an estimated 26 percent share of the $1 billion in computers sold by 1989 through outlets such as warehouse clubs, discount stores, and electronics and appliance centers. Moreover, the company had a small presence in computer specialty stores as well.

Entrepreneurs earn handsome returns from abandoned products, which are cheap and cost little to market. Many of the high costs corporations incur are avoided because entrepreneurs can work in homes, basements, warehouses, or low-rent facilities. Consider how two people from Minnesota rejuvenated Ipana toothpaste. Ipana was marketed by Bristol-Myers until 1968, when it was abandoned in favor of promoting new brands. In early 1969, two young Minnesota entrepreneurs picked up the Ipana name and devised a new formula, but packaged the product in tubes similar to those used by the former marketer. The two Minnesotans lived off a prior heavy advertising campaign for Ipana toothpaste that Bristol-Myers paid for back in the 1950s. Working in a three-room office with few workers reduced costs tremendously. Because of such an economical operation, Ipana was sold more cheaply than national brands. All these entrepreneurs had to do was put the toothpaste in the tube and distribute it. The petrified demand for Ipana turned out to be $250,000 in the first seven months of operation.

Putting an old product back on the shelf may not be without cost. New advertising themes, different packaging, or an alteration in taste or color are often introduced to adjust to a different era. The cost of these changes, however, are minimal compared to those entailed in developing new products.

Abandonment often occurs because the originator lacks the funds needed to continue nurturing the product, or feels he has better opportunities elsewhere. To the extent that a product has nostalgic value, tremendous opportunity exists for a firm that buys the rights to it. Remember the Cabbage Patch dolls' three years of fame in the mid-1980s as the nation's best-selling toys? Sales in 1984 and 1985 exceeded half a billion dollars before the dolls lost popularity and nearly vanished. The dolls are now on most toy industry lists of top-sellers, and industry analysts say the dolls have registered more than $100 million in retail sales recently. The success originating with the dolls is attributed to Hasbro Industries, which bought the production and marketing rights to Cabbage Patch from Coleco Industries in the summer of 1989. By advertising the doll heavily and increasing shipments to big toy stores, Hasbro managed to tap into the lingering strength of the Cabbage Patch name.

New users. An abandoned product may be reintroduced to new users when changes and some costs are most likely necessary. In reviving abandoned products, both new and former users often become a company's target.

> "To revive products in decline, new ways of creating value for customers must be found."

Even in the movie business, rejuvenation occurs. For example, "The Plot Against Harry," directed by Michael Roemer, was a newly discovered smash hit in 1991. The film, with Martin Priest in the title role, tells of a small-time racketeer released from prison, trying to pick up the pieces of his former illicit ventures. Ironically, when it was first released in 1969 no one thought the comedy was funny, and it was quickly withdrawn from circulation. Two decades later, it was released again and the critics fell all over themselves praising the film's black humor.

Abandoned products may be more valuable today than in the environment in which they were first introduced. Consider these examples.

With the help of videotape cassettes, Hollywood producers have become specialists in reviving movies that once failed. Lorimar, for instance, revived two movies that disappeared soon after they were released. Both "American Anthem" and "Power" were reborn as home videos months after they bombed at the box office.

The Coca-Cola Company has recently resurrected Fresca, a grapefruit-flavored drink that had been restaged several times since its introduction in 1966. Fresca went through a period of low sales and market share that culminated in its being withdrawn from virtually every market in the country. In 1985, however, the drink was reformulated with a NutraSweet base, 1 percent real grapefruit juice, and a cloudy appearance. The new product was designed to attract an upscale audience, 25 years old and older, with incomes of $30,000 and above, who were looking for a low-calorie alternative to other drinks. But it was introduced only in some areas. So in 1991 Coca-Cola began its national reintroduction.

One of the recent product trends in the toy business is the resurrection of items that appealed to an earlier generation and were then withdrawn from the market. A good example is Creepy Crawlers—plastic bugs a child makes by pouring a liquid plastic into a mold and then baking it. Originated by Mattel in 1965, this toy was successful for a few years and was then removed from the market in 1968. Mattel let the trademark expire in 1985. Subsequently, another firm, Toymax Inc., picked up the name and sold around 500,000 sets in 1992 at a price of $25 each. The new version of Creepy Crawlers is very much like the original, except that the oven has been redesigned for greater safety. Other toy-industry examples of profitable reintroductions are the G.I. Joe line, Erector Sets, and troll dolls.

Rejuvenating Declining Products and Businesses

The most common corporate strategy for a business on the wane has been a "harvest" strategy—

reduce investment, cut costs, improve cash flow, and eventually divest when income drops below cost. The strategy of harvesting a business entity, whether a division, product line, specific product, or brand, was popularized by the Boston Consulting Group.

Harvesting can be a useful strategy for an unprofitable business in decline. However, a declining business has the potential of becoming quite profitable when value is created.

The solution to declining markets is creating value. Changes in advertising, distribution, and pricing strategy have short-term effects. To revive products in decline, new ways of creating value for customers must be found. To create value, companies must monitor the changing environment and continuously adapt their businesses to their best opportunities. They must watch for sudden changes and new threats, forces and megatrends—demographic, economic, physical, technological, political, legal, social, and cultural—in the macroenvironment that may create or prevent these opportunities.

Consider Yamaha, a maker of pianos (and other goods). When the company controlled 40 percent of the global piano market, total demand was sliding by 10 percent per year. Yamaha could have labeled the piano business a "dog," then harvested and eventually divested. Instead, the company opted not to give up. Managers took a close look at the customer and the product, and found that the majority of pianos sit around idle and neglected—and out of tune most of the time. Many people own pianos, but not many owners play any more. Mastering the piano requires an investment in time, which people seem to lack nowadays. So Yamaha decided to add value to the millions of pianos already in the market by developing a sophisticated, advanced combination of digital and optical technology that can record live performances of pianists and play the compositions on the piano. The advent of this new technology has revived the piano industry as a result, while creating all kinds of possibilities.

Red meat is another example. The growing concern over the place of red meat in a healthy diet has dampened industry growth. The meat industry has had to reexamine the entire system of raising, packing, cutting, packaging, and transporting red meat, thereby addressing the health concerns that have eroded the product's image. A wide variety of marketing strategies have been employed, including television commercials, point-of-purchase programs, and print media campaigns. The National Live Stock and Meat Board and the Beef Industry Council have launched a campaign to educate consumers about the benefits of red meat. In addition, the Board has launched such point-of-purchase efforts as Meat Nutri-Facts, a program aimed at informing the consumers about specific cuts of meat, and Meat Features, a program that uses videos to stimulate interest in specific cuts of meat.

Consider also the comeback of Brylcreem. Once a top tonsorial topper for swinging guys of the 1950s, (the slogan "A little dab'll do ya" was very popular), Brylcreem managed to gain popularity in the UK in the 1980s because of the fashion trends that combined nostalgia with wet look hairstyles. To capitalize on the trend, Grey Ltd. ran a series of television spots from the 1950s. Brylcreem sales figures for the period since the relaunch are not available, but 1984 sales were 5 million units. That is equivalent to 5 percent of the 100 million tubes sold annually in the 1950s.

> "In most cases the potential of an old product is realized by an outsider, rather than by those who have had a long-term involvement with it."

Unfortunately, in most cases the potential of a product is realized by an outsider, rather than by those who have had a long-term involvement with the product. In each of the following examples, value was created by the product's new owner.

Nestlé's acquisition in January 1994 of Ward Johnson's candy products has allowed it to revive the two candy packages—notably Raisinets and Goobers—that for more than 50 years had been sold only in movie theaters. Nestlé reformulated the products, gave them new packaging, and made them into national brands with distribution to supermarkets, convenience stores, and other retailers. The company has two basic goals: to reacquaint Northeast consumers with the upgraded brands, and to introduce them to new people in the Western states.

Barbasol had not led a shaving category since the 1940s, when it was sold in tubes and jars. Production had ceased in 1953, and the brand headed toward oblivion. But in the mid-1960s Pfizer bought the company and established Barbasol in aerosol form and as a "value" label in supermarkets. In return for these efforts, Barbasol rose into the top five aerosol creams by 1979, and by 1985 had captured the number one spot.

FIVE STEPS TO REJUVENATION

Rejuvenation strategies clearly vary widely in their possibilities. Reintroducing abandoned products or reviving seriously declining ones requires managers to learn how to recognize an opportunity for injecting new life into a product.

The specific rejuvenation strategy of any firm must be tailored to its capabilities and the requirements of its macroenvironment. How does a company determine an opportunity for rejuvenation? Five steps can minimize the potential problems and increase the chances of success.

Determine the reasons for the product's abandonment or decline. Was the product abandoned because of resource constraints? Poor management? Did the product decline because of limited value?

Examine whether the forces in the macroenvironment support a rejuvenation strategy. Products today are not necessarily perceived in the same manner as in the past. So explore whether and how the product altered with changing circumstances. For example, Lucazade, a product promoted years ago as a "get-well drink" ("Lucazade aids recovery") could not be promoted as such today, given the current political and legal environment.

Examine what the product name communicates to consumers. A brand name communicates product attributes—not by an advertising message, but simply by its appearance on the product. The manner in which it is used and its relation to competitive products also communicate something.

Explore whether there is a potential segment to be reached, as well as competitors' strengths and weaknesses in that potential segment. An abandoned product can be reintroduced to previous users, if there are some who miss it. Competitors cannot compete effectively if the product has nostalgic value. Given the new market niche for the product, competitive analysis ought to reveal exactly how it relates to competition.

Examine the possibilities of creating value for customers. By monitoring the changing environment, the firm may see an opportunity for rejuvenation. The forces and megatrends in the macroenvironment—demographic, economic, physical, technological, political, legal, and sociocultural—may offer opportunities for rejuvenation.

Managers tend to place considerable importance on developing new products. Given the pitfalls of new product introduction, they might also consider rejuvenating abandoned or declining products. Product rejuvenation strategies are often simpler, cheaper, and faster, and offer handsome returns. ❐

References

"Abandoned Trademark Turns a Tidy Profit for Two Minnesotans," *Wall Street Journal,* October 27, 1969, p. 1.

Bill Abrams, "Exploiting Proven Brand Names Can Cut Risk of New Products," *Wall Street Journal*, February 18, 1982, p. 31.

S.L. Berry, "Upbeat Beef Spots Battle Red Meat's Foul Image," *Advertising Age,* October 13, 1986, p. S-12.

Booz, Allen and Hamilton, *New Products Management for the 1980s* (New York: 1982).

Arthur Bragg, "Back to the Future," *Sales and Marketing Management*, November 1986, pp. 61-62.

David Broadbent, "Giving New Life to Old Products," *Marketing,* September 17, 1980, pp. 37-38.

H. Kurt Christensen, Arnold C. Cooper, and Cornelis A. DeKluyver, "The Dog Business: A Re-examination," *Business Horizons,* November-December 1982, pp. 12-15.

Christine Donahue, "Marketers Restore Old Masters," *AdWeek's Marketing Week,* September 14, 1987, p. 1.

Mike Duff, "New Twists Needed in Marketing Red Meat," *Supermarket Business Magazine,* August 1989, pp. 17+.

Larry Edwards, "Back to the Basics," *Advertising Age,* August 20, 1987, pp. 107-110.

Betsy D. Gelb, "Strategic Planning for the Under-Dog," *Business Horizons,* November-December 1982, pp. 8-11.

Nancy Giges, "Coke Gets its Juices Flowing: Orange, Recast Fresca Ready," *Advertising Age,* April 15, 1985, p. 1.

Donald C. Hambrick and Ian C. Macmillan, "The Product Portfolio and Man's Best Friend," *California Management Review,* Fall 1982, pp. 84-95.

R.G. Hammermesh, M.J. Anderson Jr., and J.E. Harris, "Strategies for Low Market Share Businesses," *Harvard Business Review,* May-June 1978, pp. 95-102.

David S. Hopkins and Earl L. Bailey, "New Product Pressures," *Conference Board Record,* June 1971, pp. 16-24.

Philip Kotler, *Marketing Management: Analysis, Planning, Implementation, and Control,* 6th ed. (Englewood Cliffs, NJ: Prentice-Hall, 1988).

Philip Kotler, "Harvesting Strategies for Weak Products," *Business Horizons,* August 1978, pp. 15-22.

Carol Lawson, "Cabbage Patch Back in Business," *New York Times,* December 13, 1990, p. D1.

William Lazer, Mushtaq Luqmani, and Zahir Quraeshi, "Product Rejuvenation Strategies," *Business Horizons,* November-December 1984, pp. 21-28.

"New Revival: Old-Time Gum," *New York Times,* December 25, 1986, p. 45.

Kenichi Ohmae, "Getting Back to Strategy," *Harvard Business Review,* November-December 1988, pp. 149-156.

Molly O'Neill, "The Cake Box From Heaven (Brooklyn, Of Course) Is Back," *New York Times,* June 5, 1991, p. C1.

"Return of Fresca," *New York Times,* February 14, 1991, p. D4.

Bill Saporito, "Has–been Brands Go Back to Work," *Fortune,* April 28, 1986, pp. 123-124.

Eben Shapiro, "The Nostalgic Allure of Molten Plastic," *New York Times,* July 8, 1992, p. D3.

Bruce Weber, "Belatedly, the Plot Against Harry Hatches," *New York Times,* January 7, 1990, p. 13.

Laural Wentz, "Brylcreem on Comeback Trail in U.K.," *Advertising Age,* January 20, 1986, p. 41.

Steve Weiner, "New Wine in Vintage Bottles," *Forbes,* May 14, 1990, pp. 122-123.

Conrad Berenson is a professor of marketing at Baruch College, City University of New York. **Iris Mohr-Jackson** is an assistant professor of marketing at St. John's University, Jamaica, N.Y.